Promoting Corporate Citizenship:

Opportunities for Business and Civil Society Engagement

Edited by Laurie Regelbrugge

CIVICUS
World Alliance for Citizen Participation

CIVICUS is an international alliance dedicated to strengthening citizen action and civil society throughout the world.

Our vision is a worldwide community of informed, inspired, committed citizens engaged in confronting the challenges facing humanity.

CIVICUS is dedicated to pursuing a world such that:

- citizen action is a predominant feature of the political, economic and cultural life of all societies;
- private action for the public good is expressed by a rich and diverse array of organizations operating sometimes apart and sometimes in dialogue with government and business; and
- a healthy society is one in which there is an equitable relationship among citizens, their associations and foundations, business and governments.

CIVICUS's special purpose, therefore, is to help nurture the foundation, growth, protection and resourcing of citizen action throughout the world and especially in areas where participatory democracy, freedom of association of citizens and their funds for public benefit are threatened.

As a global alliance of citizens and their organizations, we help advance regional, national and international initiatives to strengthen the capacity of civil society. In partnership with our members, we are committed to:

- strengthening the visibility and understanding of civil society;
- working to develop a more supportive environment of laws, policies, and regulations;
- developing permanent, self-sustaining, and creative resource mechanisms;
- having an open forum, serving to facilitate and establish cross-sectoral dialogue, exchange information, develop a common understanding and shared identity, solidarity, cooperation, and communication within civil society from various regions, and promote a common vision about the role of civil society.

For further information about CIVICUS membership, publications, advocacy, and meetings:

CIVICUS: World Alliance for Citizen Participation
919 18th Street NW, Third Floor
Washington, DC 20006
U.S.A.
Tel: (202) 331-8518
Fax: (202) 331-8774
www.civicus.org

ISBN 1-929842-00-7

Manufactured in the United States of America.

Table of Contents

Preface *Laurie Regelbrugge, Editor* v

Foreword *Kumi Naidoo* vii

Chapter 1 Introducing the CIVICUS Corporate Engagement Project
Manuel Arango 1

Chapter 2 Business and Civil Society: Reflections on Roles, Responsibilities, and Opportunities at the Dawn of a New Century
Laurie Regelbrugge 5

Chapter 3 Mapping Corporate Citizenship: A Survey of Global, National, and Local Initiatives
Maxwell Brem, under direction of Chris Pinney 27

Chapter 4 Business Partners for Development: Vision, History, and Potential
Nigel Twose and Amanda Blakeley 71

Chapter 5 The Learning and Sharing Process: Why Is Partnership between Sectors such a Challenge?
Ros Tennyson and Alina Zyszkowski 81

Chapter 6 Capturing the Lessons of Partnership and Practice: A Review of Corporate-NGO Partnerships in Asia Pacific
Tadashi Yamamoto 89

Chapter 7 Capturing the Lessons of Partnership and Practice: Initiatives to Promote Corporate Engagement in Latin America
Marisol Pagés and Nelson Stratta 97

Chapter 8 An Initiative to Promote Corporate Engagement in North America
Peter Shiras and Roberto Senderowitsch 105

Chapter 9 Business and Civil Society Organizations: Toward a New Partnership
Christopher Pinney 111

Chapter 10 Aspirations for Advancing Corporate Citizenship in the Next Millennium
Rajesh Tandon 115

Resources on Business and Civil Society Engagement 121

Preface

CIVICUS is pleased to present *Promoting Corporate Citizenship: Opportunities for Business and Civil Society Engagement* as a product of its Corporate Engagement Project. This publication describes our rationale for undertaking the corporate engagement project, provides ideas and resources, and offers perspectives from practitioners who are working in many parts of the world to build constructive relationships between business and civil society organizations.

The authors were chosen from a broad array of CIVICUS partners. Some authors are CIVICUS members, others are not. We invited their contributions to this publication on the basis of their experience with business and community engagement. Authors were given little time to prepare their chapters because of the production schedule we had to meet to have the publication completed for the CIVICUS World Assembly in Manila, Philippines, in September 1999. We are deeply grateful to all authors for their willingness to prepare and review chapters, toiling under intense deadline pressure to deliver insightful pieces.

Many other CIVICUS members, board members, regional affiliates, and partners, well beyond the authors represented herein, have experience with corporate citizenship and business-community engagement. While we could not present every initiative in this publication, we hope the cases and resources discussed here merely whet readers' appetites for more of this subject matter. I also wish to acknowledge the important contribution made by those CIVICUS members who have serious questions about the utility and desirability of corporate engagement. Their critical challenges and comments are important ingredients in any forward progress, achievements, and positive results.

On behalf of the CIVICUS board of directors and staff, I convey our deepest thanks to Manuel Arango and the CIVICUS Corporate Engagement Task Force members, a list of whom is on the inside back cover. They have launched a thoughtful exploration of corporate citizenship that will benefit our communities, locally and globally, by inspiring corporations and civil society organizations to improve their practices. We thank Chris Pinney and his colleagues at Imagine, a program of the Canadian Centre for Philanthropy, for facilitating the task force's work.

Funding and strong encouragement for this publication came from the American Express Foundation and The Hitachi Foundation. Both institutions have been centrally involved in the CIVICUS Corporate Engagement Project, providing financial and substantive support along with their direct involvement. We deeply appreciate their commitment to achieving highly effective, mutually beneficial business-civil society partnerships, and we have learned a great deal from their participation in this work with us.

We also acknowledge and appreciate the financial support and direct involvement of the World Bank Group, through the Business Partners for Development (BPD) Initiative's Knowledge Resource Group (KRG). CIVICUS's relationship with the World Bank Group and the Prince of Wales Business Leaders Forum in the KRG is an important component of its corporate engagement work.

This publication would not have been possible without the generous support CIVICUS receives from several donors. We therefore gratefully acknowledge the continued support of the Charles Stewart Mott Foundation, the Ford Foundation, the W.K. Kellogg Foundation, the Rockefeller Brothers Fund, and the David and Lucile Packard Foundation, among others. Their support for CIVICUS staff and operations ensures the organization's viability.

We are grateful to Gary Kessler for his patient, thorough, and effective editing. He, too, had difficult deadlines to meet, but met them cheerfully and professionally. Marian Bollinger and her colleagues at Artech Graphics provided high quality, customer-friendly service in designing and printing this publication, which I underscore as one manifestation of the company's corporate citizenship.

The final thanks go to colleagues here at CIVICUS—staff members and interns—who make things happen under any and all conditions. This publication is a product of the strong foundation laid by Miklós Marschall and of Kumi Naidoo's deep vision, pragmatism, and enthusiasm for strengthening civil society. Jo Render has contributed invaluable skills and expertise in managing the Corporate Engagement Project and developing the partnership with BPD. Without Jo's leadership, we would not be in a position to share any lessons learned. Angela Lane provided critical production coordination. Alina Zyszkowski provided important insights from her experience and from the KRG activities. Marylin Coicou provided research assistance. Elizabeth Stoneham, Janet Malabarba Oliver, Juan Villalobos, and Lucianna Winters kept other CIVICUS activities running smoothly while some of us were preoccupied with this publication. Statements of thanks are insufficient to acknowledge the valuable role that these people play in bringing CIVICUS projects and products to fruition. I extend my deepest gratitude to my colleagues.

Laurie Regelbrugge, Editor

Foreword

Kumi Naidoo

CIVICUS's mission is integral to the ambitious Third CIVICUS World Assembly theme: "Towards a New Civil Society: The Changing Roles of Civil Society Organizations, Business, and Government." To address this theme successfully, we must explore how business and civil society organizations interact. What are the possibilities, the pitfalls, and promising examples that offer effective new ways of working together and working independently? Considering the dramatic increase in business activity and growing influence of business organizations, the time is right for discussion about what responsibilities coincide with the growing power and influence that the business sector wields. While debate about the roles of society's three sectors is crucial, we must also determine how these roles are to be implemented by individual businesses and civil society organizations.

There are many skeptics within civil society, and indeed within business and government as well, that question whether engagement of the business sector in the social sector can yield true progress or whether it simply co-opts civil society organizations. These cautions are no doubt understandable given that relationships between civil society organizations and companies either have been adversarial or have largely been at the level of cash contributions by business to those nonprofit organizations whose goals they supported. Yet, a categorical dismissal of all business engagement fails to recognize the positive power that can be harnessed from within the business sector that includes, but goes way beyond, cash contributions.

Civil society activists have also come to realize that a growing number of businesses are striving for more socially responsible ways to conduct business and that there are now some cases where social improvements have been brought about by businesses working in partnership either with government, civil society organizations, or both. Just as there is vast diversity among civil society organizations, businesses—though all driven to a large extent by the profit motive—vary broadly in their approach to business practices and corporate citizenship. As we approach the new millennium, considering the breadth and scope of business activity and its influence in development and globalization, the question is whether civil society can afford not to engage the business sector.

It would be somewhat irresponsible today if civil society organizations at the local, national, and international level did not develop an approach on how to engage the business sector. Engagement does not have to mean cooption; neither does it have to mean that the two parties will not differ and disagree on several matters of interest. However, if the position of the poor and socially marginalized can be improved, or if the development challenges facing a community, a country, or the world at large can be addressed by engaging business, then civil society organizations are duty bound to do this.

It is important to note that when we say that the human being or the citizen (used in a nonlegalistic manner) is the building block of civil society, this offers us the opportunity of a valuable bridge across the three sectors. First, we can agree that civil society organizations include such institutions as nongovernmental organizations (NGOs), voluntary organizations, nonprofits, religious bodies, trade unions, social movements, neighborhood groups, and so on. These are citizen-inspired organizational entities that advance specific causes or interests of their members and supporters. Second, while a big corporation or a government institution itself is not part of civil society, the persons who work within these institutions have the opportunity to embrace civil society in the places they live, worship, and find recreation. There is an African proverb that says, "I am, because you are," which underscores the idea that we find our humanity and our own dignity in the relationships we build in the communities where we reside. Therefore, as is currently the case, thousands of people who work full time for government or for a business entity are involved in myriad ways in activities that serve to promote the interests of communities through nonprofit associations of various types.

This argument does not seek to negate the structural inequalities that exist; the different power positions of different sectors based on wealth, access, and influence; and so on. Indeed, all of this is important, and good relationships will only be built if these inherent contradictions are acknowledged in an open, candid, and honest manner. Acknowledging these differences should not lead us to a position where the three sectors withdraw into their own parochial corners and ignore the others' existence. Thankfully, today even powerful governments have recognized that they have to engage with civil society organizations if they are to achieve their societal goals.

In a recent conference in Japan, which explored the question of NGO-Corporate Partnership in the Asia Pacific region, I made the point that we need to recognize that there is a gradation of relationships that can exist between the

"Considering the dramatic increase in business activity and growing influence of business organizations, the time is right for discussion about what responsibilities coincide with the growing power and influence that the business sector wields."

business sector and civil society organizations. First there is interaction, then there is engagement, and finally the highest form of relationship is partnership, which can have a programmatic focus. We also noted that the reasons why civil society organizations and businesses choose to develop relationships can vary from situation to situation and often might not be driven solely by philanthropy, charity, or benevolence. But this should not be a problem for civil society organizations, provided such business interests are declared up front. If the business partner derives direct or indirect benefit, a longer-term commitment is probably likely. As for the civil society organization, it will have to examine whether any principle is being sacrificed by entering such relationships. I suspect that, provided the interests of the communities we seek to serve are being advanced and that no dishonorable deals are done behind the scenes, such relationships should be mutually beneficial and publicly defendable.

This Foreword begins to explain why CIVICUS is interested in corporate citizenship and what we have learned about what promise corporate citizenship has for improving society. This publication seeks to share what we and many others in the world have learned in efforts to promote positive relationships between businesses and civil society organizations.

RATIONALE FOR THE CIVICUS CORPORATE ENGAGEMENT TASK FORCE

In 1998 CIVICUS launched its Corporate Engagement Task Force and decided to have a business and community engagement stream of programming in the 1999 CIVICUS World Assembly. These decisions reflected a growing awareness among the CIVICUS board and members that to advance its own work, civil society had to develop new ways of engaging and working with the business sector. These relationships would have to take many forms, and they would have to identify the promise and potential of business and community engagement.

With the results of the task force's first year of work, and with the prospect of broader debate at the 1999 World Assembly, CIVICUS is more committed than ever to creating a space in which civil society organizations and businesses can explore their respective strengths and mutual interests in building healthy, viable communities. Several assumptions guide this work.

First, we believe that a growing number of businesses are striving to be responsible companies throughout their operations. They try to treat their employees fairly and with appropriate benefits, they try to use natural resources responsibly, and they try to be good neighbors within communities where they operate.

Another assumption is that civil society and business have not yet developed many partnerships through which each partner contributes from its respective, comparative strengths. The most common model of partnership we see today casts businesses as the resource providers and civil society organizations as the resource seekers, implying a one-way flow of resources. This model undervalues both sectors' assets. It also fails to disclose how each sector, and the larger society, benefits from the relationship. Many of the advancements in corporate behavior in the past were rooted either in adversarial relations between the sectors, which often led to complicated government regulation, or in unilateral action by companies. We believe that adversarial relations will continue to play a role in the future. We also believe that civil society, and society in general, has more to gain from tapping a broader range of business-community interaction, not least of which is self-interest. After all, eliminating adverse behavior alone does not begin to tap the range of ways that companies can contribute to development through their intellectual, human, financial, and organizational capital.

A third assumption is that well beyond civil society it is also in the business sector's interest to eliminate deleterious business practices. Rogue businesses undermine the efforts of reputable, responsible companies. Such practices may allow some owners and even a few consumers to benefit, sometimes handsomely, in the short run. However, the whole society suffers in the long run when companies gain an advantage through negligent or irresponsible actions. Law-abiding companies have as much interest as civil society does in eliminating irresponsible business practices to avoid unfair competition and to prevent cumbersome and sometimes unnecessary regulation.

A final assumption is that civil society also must change as a result of the influence of new partnerships with the business sector. In this new context of larger, more pervasive business and smaller, or less resource-rich, government, civil society's structure and approaches must be redesigned creatively to take advantage of the learning and opportunities available through strategic alliances. While we definitely want to see civil society positively influencing business

> *"There is an African proverb that says, 'I am, because you are,' which underscores the idea that we find our humanity and our own dignity in the relationships we build in the communities where we reside."*

practices, perhaps the most important ambition is to learn how to strengthen civil society through its engagement with the business sector.

THE WORLD ASSEMBLY AS A FORUM FOR INCREASING AWARENESS AND DEBATE

The World Assembly provides a valuable opportunity to launch discussions with the aim of achieving constructive steps forward. We seek new and deeper kinds of business and community interaction, both within the institutional contexts of business enterprises and civil society organizations and through the individual people who work in these sectors. CIVICUS's efforts are not designed to dismiss or overlook deleterious business practice. On the contrary, CIVICUS and many of its partners are keenly aware of negative business practices that have harmed people, hurt the environment, and impeded development. Instead, CIVICUS offers a forum where these two sectors can meet and jointly arrive at more constructive responses and deliberate plans for positive change. Throughout the twentieth century, civil society has played an important role in challenging, and sometimes pressuring, business to improve its practices. As a new century and millennium dawn, civil society has the opportunity and obligation to develop a broader array of tools and channels for working with companies to advance social, economic, and environmental development.

Sessions designed to address business and community engagement are included throughout the Manila World Assembly program, although the most concentrated treatment is in a plenary session entitled "Considerations for Business and Community Engagement." This session will frame the topic and will offer a few primary questions to guide debate. Representatives from business, civil society, and government will respond to these questions and give their general reactions to the position paper that is circulated to the CIVICUS membership for comment before the World Assembly.

Breakout group sessions are designed to be highly interactive and to foster discussion about concrete experience. Facilitators and panelists come from corporations, corporate foundations, civil society organizations, and government agencies. Among the sessions planned for the Assembly are: Building Successful Partnerships with Business, Making the Case for Corporate Citizenship, Social Entrepreneurship, The Role of Intermediaries, A Case Study of the Business Partners for Development Initiative, A Case Study of the Institute for Development Research's Project, Measuring Corporate Citizenship—Business and Civil Society Perspectives, Global Initiatives to Encourage Corporate Citizenship—The CIVICUS Corporate Engagement Project, Role of Governments in Encouraging and Enabling Corporate Citizenship.

There are also sessions that will occur in the Governance and Social Cohesion thematic tracks of the World Assembly: Shareholders versus Stakeholders? Corporate Governance in a Global Economy, Regulating Business in a Global Economy, The Workplace as Community, and Global Business—Global Culture.

The Business and Community Engagement sessions seek to present what is possible and what is preferable in business-NGO partnerships while addressing the larger theme of defining the appropriate future roles for civil society, business, and government. The sessions were selected for their treatment of fundamental issues and for their attention to emerging opportunities and trends. The list of sessions is just a beginning in what we hope will be a long-standing effort to address this challenge comprehensively and strategically.

PERSPECTIVES ON PROMOTING CORPORATE CITIZENSHIP TO ADVANCE LEARNING

As part of the preparation for the 1999 World Assembly, CIVICUS decided to publish some of the perspectives and experience it has come across through the work of its task force, members, and partners. This publication, *Promoting Corporate Citizenship: Opportunities for Business and Civil Society Engagement*, was conceived to share a vision for what business and civil society relationships can become and to deliver some concrete information from several different contexts about how to work together effectively.

The framework for presenting the information is, first, to offer a rationale for why CIVICUS is interested in business and civil society engagement and interaction. Second, the publication seeks to provide an overview of the corporate citizenship field's landscape, so that CIVICUS's work is taken in context. Next, we seek to deliver some lessons that practitioners have learned in pursuing business and civil society partnerships. Because the regional and cul-

---

"Law-abiding companies have as much interest as civil society does in eliminating irresponsible business practices to avoid unfair competition and to prevent cumbersome and sometimes unnecessary regulation."

---

tural contexts are so very important in relationships, we then feature examples from a global initiative—Business Partners for Development—and examples from three other regions of the world where business and civil society partnerships are in varying stages of development: Asia Pacific, Latin America, and North America. These examples are by no means exhaustive, but they illustrate the issues, growing interest, and varied experience in these kinds of partnerships. Finally, we present perspectives on the future of corporate citizenship and business-civil society partnerships and discuss options for CIVICUS's work in this area.

We invited several practitioner-authors to share their experience and advice. Their chapters offer reflections, opinions, and questions about corporate citizenship, and they offer practical information about business and civil society partnerships from their direct experience in such partnerships. Their chapters feature experience and examples from many parts of the world. Not one of these authors will say that these relationships are easy. By the same token, not one of these authors has concluded that these relationships are not worth the effort. On the contrary, their experience seems to suggest that business-civil society relationships are perhaps the single most important strategy of the future. They are realistic in their appraisal of the promise, limitations, and pitfalls of forging these kinds of relationships across the sectors. Their reflections and practical suggestions provide valuable insights that may help others among us pursue partnerships more effectively from the start.

In chapter 1, Manuel Arango provides background on and insight from the CIVICUS Corporate Engagement Task Force, on which he serves as chairperson. As a business owner and chief executive and as a founder of a crucial civil society organization in Mexico, Manuel Arango understands better than most what opportunities and operating constraints each sector faces. He also understands their interdependence and comparative strengths. His vision and pragmatism have laid an important foundation for the Corporate Engagement Task Force to contribute something of value to the debate.

Chapter 2 offers a vision for corporate citizenship and for business and civil society as key strategic partners in the future. This vision, and its related practical suggestions for building these partnerships, comes from Laurie Regelbrugge's experience with The Hitachi Foundation and with development NGOs. For many years she worked on teams responsible for developing programs and internal channels for Hitachi's global corporate citizenship efforts. She and colleagues developed many business-community partnerships while also studying the approaches of many other corporations. Laurie's experience has been further infused by her current work as the chief operating officer and general manager at CIVICUS.

Chapter 3 presents a broad view and analysis of the corporate citizenship landscape compiled by Maxwell Brem, under the direction of Chris Pinney and colleagues in the Imagine Project of the Canadian Centre for Philanthropy. Chris Pinney and Imagine were chosen to facilitate the work of the CIVICUS Corporate Engagement Task Force based on their experience with the business and civil society sectors and their knowledge of global trends in corporate citizenship. The team is now soliciting comments globally on several strategic options for moving the task force's work forward.

In chapter 4, Nigel Twose and Amanda Blakeley of the World Bank Group offer the history of the Business Partners in Development (BPD) Initiative that is promoting trisector partnerships (business, government, and civil society) to improve development in countries around the world. Though initiated by the World Bank Group, BPD has always been "demand driven" in that it was created to respond to an urgent need among global businesses to find ways to work more effectively with government and community partners.

Chapter 5 features an honest account of the trials and tribulations of partnership and the potential for learning from the BPD. It is written by Ros Tennyson of the Prince of Wales Business Leaders Forum and Alina Zyszkowski of the BPD's Knowledge Resource Group, for which CIVICUS hosts the secretariat. Ros Tennyson is a seasoned veteran in the field of business-community partnerships, and she has designed and contributed valuable tools that help novices navigate through the difficulties that dissuade most partnership seekers early on. Among them is a book called *Managing Partnerships.*

In chapter 6, Tadashi Yamamoto, president of the Japan Center for International Exchange (JCIE), presents a summary of the findings from a two-year project to compile case studies of business-community partnerships in the Asia Pacific region. Tadashi Yamamoto and his colleagues in this project built on their years of experience and the vast diversity within the region. They selected global and local firms, and global, regional, and local NGOs as their targets of inquiry. The resulting case studies, available in a JCIE pub-

> *"Ultimately, the quality of business and community engagement depends on the quality and diversity of the perspectives considered and the commitment to explore these issues constructively, with an eye toward ever improving practice."*

lication, offer valuable insights about the promise and limitations of business-civil society partnerships.

Chapter 7, by Marisol Pagés of the Esquel Group Foundation and Nelson Stratta of Grupo Esquel Uruguay, provides an important perspective on just how deeply the historical development of the three sectors in Latin America influences the development of partnerships. They underscore the key role both history and culture continue to play in the ability of the business sector, government, and civil society to work together. While there are many difficulties yet to be overcome, Marisol Pagés and Nelson Stratta are optimistic that cross-sector relationships can do a better job delivering the public good and healthy communities than any of the three sectors can do independently.

In chapter 8 by Peter Shiras and Roberto Senderowitsch, both of CIVICUS North America and Independent Sector, CIVICUS in North America—which includes members in Mexico, Canada, and the United States—presents preliminary plans for a corporate citizenship project. The impetus for this project came from the realization that many companies operating in the region do not have transnational strategies or activities. In fact, many have very different practices in each of these three countries. With a complex array of regulations and administrative barriers within the increasing scenario of regional cooperation in which the North American Free Trade Agreement was created, CIVICUS in North America seeks to contribute to the development of a regional framework for corporate citizenship.

Chapter 9, by Chris Pinney, highlights the history of business and civil society interaction and summarizes current efforts to promote partnerships. He describes the status of the CIVICUS corporate engagement project, and identifies the options that exist for future work by CIVICUS and others.

In chapter 10, Rajesh Tandon, chair of the CIVICUS board of directors and executive director of the Society for Participatory Research in Asia (PRIA), presents the imperative for civil society, business, and government to learn how to work together more effectively in addressing and delivering the public good. Rajesh Tandon acknowledges that these sectors must at times work independently and at other times collectively to achieve these objectives. He favors relationship building and partnerships as the easiest way to practice and improve skills in working together.

Ultimately, the quality of business and community engagement depends on the quality and diversity of the perspectives considered and the commitment to explore these issues constructively, with an eye toward ever improving practice. We will succeed if we attract representatives from civil society, business, and government to explore together how we might build more effective working relationships to address the larger goal of more equitable, humane social, economic, and environmental development. We hope this publication contributes positively toward this larger goal.

Finally, I wish to acknowledge and thank Laurie Regelbrugge, CIVICUS chief operating officer and general manager, who served as editor of this publication in her first weeks at CIVICUS. Her contribution was invaluable in making this project possible in an insanely short space of time. Laurie brought experience, integrity, and professionalism to this project, for which we are deeply grateful. My deepest gratitude thus goes out to Laurie and all the members of the CIVICUS global secretariat, recognizing that without their commitment, energy, and effort this publication would not have seen the light of day.

Kumi Naidoo joined CIVICUS as secretary general and chief executive officer in 1998. Previously, he was the founding executive director of the South African National NGO Coalition (SANGOCO), the umbrella agency for the NGO community in South Africa. Mr. Naidoo initiated and led a wide range of education, development, and social justice initiatives within South Africa. He is currently a member of the Commonwealth Foundation's NGO Advisory Committee. Expelled from school in South Africa at the age of 15 as a result of his anti-apartheid activities, Mr. Naidoo is a Rhodes Scholar and holds degrees in politics and law, including a doctoral degree in political sociology at Oxford University.

Introducing the CIVICUS Corporate Engagement Project

1

Manuel Arango

"Goal: Increased and stronger partnerships among corporate, government, and civil society institutions."

A BIT OF HISTORY

When it began independent programming in 1994, CIVICUS was faced with a dilemma. It was founded with a mission as broad as "strengthening civil society around the world" and a constituency that would therefore need to span both the globe and the incredible diversity of institutions and individuals working within and on behalf of civil society. With this broad mission, CIVICUS had to determine a focused course of action that would add value to the amazing work already being done by its members and partners.

I was honored to be a part of its first World Assembly, held in Mexico City in January 1995, and I watched CIVICUS take an incredibly risky and fascinating first step: to ask its constituents directly what the goals and direction of the organization should be. They responded enthusiastically with five major goals for the organization, one of which is listed above: increased and stronger partnerships among corporate, government, and civil society institutions.

In all of its programming since 1995, CIVICUS has made the goal of strengthening intersectoral partnerships a foundation for its work. However, this particular goal has not proven easy to achieve. Each meeting of members, regional discussion, and project task force has had to face skepticism and suspicion that exist among the three sectors, including between civil society and the business sector. This is true even within CIVICUS's own membership, an alliance and public space where one would hope that the belief in a common mission would help parties lay these suspicions aside in an effort to move constructively beyond them.

"To give work and a decent life to the growing world population, development must certainly continue. However, to assure that this development is effective and is indeed 'progress,' it must be sustainable and equitable, which implies a balance between the creation of wealth, its use and distribution, and the assurance at the same time of its continuity."

THE CIVICUS CORPORATE ENGAGEMENT PROJECT

In looking more closely at our members and in listening to them, we found an incredible diversity of experience in creating or participating in effective business-NGO partnerships. Some have made partnership-building a staple of their programs and the way they work, and they have developed a level of sophistication that is enviable from any point of view. Conversely, some of our civil society members have continued to hold the business sector at arms' length, treating business firms with caution for their role in contributing to the degradation of the planet and the people that live on it, while admitting at the same time their importance in creating wealth and employment. How to reconcile the two is the question CIVICUS had to ask itself as well as whether there would be value in trying.

Early in 1998, the CIVICUS Board of Directors and a few of its corporate foundation members, particularly The Hitachi Foundation and American Express Philanthropic Program, discussed ideas on the potential for developing a project that would explore ways to promote effective business-civil society partnerships and collaboration on a global level. Some of the ideas have proven to be the key questions many leading organizations in this field—Business for Social Responsibility (USA), the Prince of Wales Business Leaders Forum (U.K.), and Philippine Business for Social Progress—have been grappling with for years.

- Who are we trying to reach—just civil society, just the business sector, or both?
- What message do we want to convey—a message about corporate citizenship, a message about corporate social responsibility, a message about creating effective partnerships, or all three?
- How can CIVICUS build on what is already happening in other organizations? How can CIVICUS add value to these programs? What aspect of the challenge is CIVICUS most well-suited to pursue?

> ***"We have come to realize in this era of globalization that no individual sector can face and resolve these problems on its own. It will take the best that all sectors have to offer to meet this challenge."***

After I had chaired two meetings of an international task force on corporate engagement, the answers to these questions were clear to me. CIVICUS is in a unique position to:

- Convene both sectors on a global level, creating the space for a dialogue that allows for increased understanding between the sectors;
- Communicate to all sectors in all regions that good citizenship, including corporate citizenship, is a requirement for our world today, and work with the business and civil society sectors to bring this about;
- Bring together the expertise of CIVICUS members and partners in building effective partnerships, and assist their efforts to share their experience with a global audience;
- Create tools for both the business sector and civil society to better understand each other, particularly the disparate strengths and opportunities of each, and to explore ways of working together that will be positive for both sectors and for the communities that are home to both;
- Tap into the creative energies of both sectors and help them explore ways to increase their own effectiveness by working together and sharing their skills and their resources;
- Explore with our business partners the opportunity for setting global standards of conduct, standards that are formed in cooperation with both the business sector and civil society.

THE OUTCOME

It is hard to say precisely what challenges we will face in tackling these issues. Some of them are already apparent from the task force discussions, where even the decision on the best language to use—corporate citizenship, corporate social responsibility, or corporate engagement—was preceded by heated debate. But the debate is as important as the result. It has proven to me that CIVICUS is respected as a forum for open dialogue, and that it is an organization that has proven itself by tackling the issues critical to the survival and development of our societies.

What it has also shown is that CIVICUS cannot succeed in its broad mission without looking at this issue in depth. This depth will help us act to reconcile and resolve the challenges we face in any of the following circumstances:

- When a business firm is given an award for corporate citizenship in one country while pursuing some of the most negligent and harmful practices in another,
- When civil society organizations feel free to ask a business firm for a check but have no idea about or interest in how to tap into the firm's management and marketing skills,
- When civil society organizations alert communities around the world of adverse business behavior without correspondingly highlighting promising practices that other business firms undertake, and
- When there are models of the most creative and innovative partnerships in one community that go unnoticed by the rest of the world.

I have had the tremendous opportunity to participate actively in the best of these worlds: business and civil society. I have watched many of my colleagues in business doing the same as they become involved in building their communities with their fellow citizens. We now face the challenge of drawing on the best of these worlds in joint efforts to combat some of the worst problems humanity has ever faced. We have come to realize in this era of globalization that no individual sector can face and resolve these problems on its own. It will take the best that all sectors have to offer to meet this challenge. To give work and a decent life to the growing world population, development must certainly continue. However, to assure that this development is effective and is indeed "progress," it must be sustainable and equitable, which implies a balance between the creation of wealth, its use and distribution, and the assurance at the same time of its continuity. Achieving such development requires appropriate actions by the business and civil society sectors, sometimes acting independently and sometimes in concert.

Manuel Arango is a member of the CIVICUS Board of Directors, and serves as chairperson of its Corporate Engagement Task Force. He is the founder and honorary lifetime chairman of the Centro Mexicano para la Filantropía (CEMEFI), an organization dedicated to promoting and facilitating the work of nonprofit organizations in Mexico. In addition, he is cofounder and partner of CIFRA, a general retailing business, and founder and chairman of a real estate development company in Mexico.

2 Business and Civil Society: Reflections on Roles, Responsibilities, and Opportunities at the Dawn of a New Century

Laurie Regelbrugge

Global commerce, communications, and mobility (by choice or necessity) have transformed the world in a very short time. These changes demand new, relevant skills, knowledge, approaches, institutions, and relationships, particularly with respect to the role corporations play in society. The turn of the millennium is a time to challenge companies to achieve ever higher standards of conduct and involvement in human development, and it is in their interest to do so.

It is an exciting time to promote corporate citizenship and engagement in civil society. More than ever before, it is possible to achieve consistent, high standards of corporate citizenship throughout the global operations of companies. Communications technologies provide tools for firms and communities worldwide to guide and monitor corporate behavior and its influence in society. The growing power of the commercial sector is reason enough to advance corporate citizenship practice. Yet, the vast opportunities to draw on corporate expertise and resources in strengthening our communities are even greater incentive for engagement.

Corporate activities, independently and collectively, and the influence of financial markets raise the stakes for corporate citizenship. In the last decade of the twentieth century, turbulent financial markets have caused debilitating economic crises in most parts of the world, particularly in Asia, Latin America, eastern and central Europe, and Africa. These crises have challenged civil society organizations, companies, and governments to find new ways of working together to mitigate the harsh effects of such crises. Indeed, the crises have highlighted the need for such cross-sector collaboration.

As we build the knowledge, relationships, and institutions we need in the next millennium, we also need the will and means to conserve and stimulate the world's social and environmental diversity. This rich diversity is evidence that there are many ways to think about, approach, and solve challenges we face. Our diversity is also the foundation for future development.

Achieving a healthy global society requires that corporate, civil society, and government actors find appropriate ways to interact, collaborate, and exercise their respective independent roles. As we try to adjust to our radically changing global community, while striving to maintain the creativity, diversity, and integrity of the world's people and environment, the corporate sector can be a strong ally, but only if we work to engage companies substantively and deliberately in building and strengthening society.

What then are the rights, responsibilities, and forums we need to build and sustain a healthy global society and local communities in the new millennium? What is the proper relationship among government, corporations, and civil society organizations? What role do we want and need the private sector to play?

This chapter explores how corporations and civil society organizations (CSOs) are transforming their relationships, and it presents thoughts on what is possible through their interaction. Several specific questions are addressed. What is the intersection of corporate and civil society interests? What assets and abilities (for example, financial management, strategic planning, fundraising) do corporations have that can strengthen civil society, how can these resources be mobilized, and why should these resources be mobilized to strengthen civil society? What assets and abilities do CSOs offer corporations that would promote collaboration and foster corporate engagement in strengthening civil society? What kinds of relationships and practices are most desirable? What tools can help us understand which practices and relationships are more effective than others? What roles do we need corporations to play in society in the next century and beyond?

INTRODUCTION AND OVERVIEW

Society's Three Sectors All Have Roles to Play

During this century, the private sector commercialized many of the innovations that fuel the global economy. Few would argue this point. However, we may not appreciate important roles played by society's two other sectors. Government, often within its defense interests, funded much of the research and development of the "technology era." Civil society has played critical roles in dispersing the benefits of innovations more widely, highlighting issues needing public attention, and supporting citizen action in response to human rights atrocities, adverse environmental practices, and social dislocation.

Thus there is a tacit division of labor among society's three primary sectors. However, at no level (local, national, regional, or global) have we fully resolved whether this is a desirable, or preferred, division of labor for

> *"More than ever before, it is possible to achieve consistent, high standards of corporate citizenship throughout the global operations of companies. Communications technologies provide tools for firms and communities worldwide to guide and monitor corporate behavior and its influence in society."*

the future, nor whether it is sustainable. Nor have we crafted our systems to ensure that this division of labor can be fulfilled effectively. The tensions and dynamism within these sectors, for better and for worse, defy rigid demarcations. Nevertheless, each sector has particular strengths. Building effective, equitable, just societies requires that we become more adept at understanding and drawing on these talents in our formal institutions and our informal public action.

The private for-profit sector will enter the next millennium with unprecedented size and influence. Corporations exercise vast control over the world's wealth and resources, making them powerful forces in society. Their global reach defies control or regulation by any single nation state and allows corporations to act as global players. Yet their operations must adhere to local and national laws and regulations. This means that an intimate relationship between companies and communities remains. Does corporate citizenship need to expand commensurately with the expansion of corporate action and influence globally? Does corporate citizenship need to maintain a local character that is appropriate to communities where companies have operations? What roles do we need corporations to play in society in the next century and beyond?

Long-term corporate self-interest alone dictates the need for actions and investments that are socially and environmentally responsible and appropriate. Companies thrive when there are people who have the capacity and desire to consume. Companies have the best prospects in thriving communities. Considering the extent to which corporate actions influence national and community fortunes and the availability of resources for sustenance and development, it is clear that building vibrant communities and a healthy civil society in the twenty-first century require the profound, strategic involvement of the private for-profit sector. How do companies engage effectively to strengthen society? How do they bring their core competencies to bear on critical social and environmental issues and embrace the cultures and values that exist in places they operate?

Civil society organizations also enjoy the prospect of being both global and local in their action and influence. Events in recent years have underscored the value of having a nimble sector that can mobilize resources and organize quickly to respond to new challenges, such as the AIDS epidemic, or to address recurring issues like famine. Civil society is well suited to participate alongside the private sector and government in strengthening communities, protecting the environment, and creating opportunities for human growth and development.

While much of the history of relations between corporations and civil society is best characterized as either adversarial or superficial, by the mid-1980s many corporations realized they had to become more strategic in their community involvement and they had to form new partnerships. Likewise, civil society organizations increasingly recognized that their knowledge, constituencies, and actions could, through partnerships and collaboration, contribute to more responsible corporate action, more effective government, and stronger communities.

The three sectors are already interdependent. In most of the world the government and for-profit sectors dwarf the civil society sector in size, stature, and resources. Still, CSOs raised awareness and prompted action to address such issues as AIDS, apartheid, human rights, environmental protection and conservation, and famine. CSOs serve many of society's research and development functions, diagnosing problems and then designing and testing strategies for addressing them.

Twentieth Century Trends in the Three Sectors

The twentieth century witnessed vast growth in the stature and scope of commercial activity. Entrepreneurs found ways to commoditize all sorts of things. The rapid pace of technological development fueled corporate proliferation. Innovations in communications and travel made the "global village" and the global economy realities. Toward the end of the century, as authoritarian systems and centrally planned economies folded in favor of free market democracies, it became clear that the corporate world wielded ever increasing influence in society, globally and locally.

Coinciding with this tremendous increase in corporations' control over resources, wealth, and influence, there was mounting pressure for corporations to conduct their activities responsibly. Why? The prospect of unbridled capitalism makes many people as nervous as the prospect of totalitarianism.

As market-based activity expanded, corporate citizenship gained currency in discussions about how best to build and promote healthy public life and communities. The nature and extent of a corporation's citizenship and responsibilities are matters of great debate and variation. Still, there is growing acceptance that companies must play an increasingly active, strategic role in supporting civil society, and it is in their business interest to do so.

The corporate sector was not the only sector to be transformed. The government and nonprofit sectors also changed dramatically in the twentieth century.

One might say the government sector waxed and waned. At one end of the spectrum were the communist regimes. They tested the feasibility of single sector societies in which government controlled social services and owned and controlled the means of production. The resulting huge bureaucracies typically did a few things well, such as defense, and did most things less effectively, and often poorly. Most of these regimes have now given way to democratic-style governments and market-based economies.

We also witnessed the proliferation of countries as colonial empires collapsed, spawning all sorts of smaller independent nation states. These independence movements, which occurred throughout the century, transformed governance in most regions—Africa, Asia, Europe, Latin America, and the Arab World. The role and capacity of government grew in many parts of the world. Yet, by the end of the century there was an overall decline in the capacity of government to provide for the well-being of citizens. In most countries we are now struggling to determine the most appropriate role for the public sector.

The end of World War II launched the era of international organizations, which have added new forums for intergovernmental relations and cross-sector relations. These multilateral organizations have played increasingly important roles in globalizing standards of behavior for government, and have also contributed, albeit to a lesser extent, to discussions on global standards for corporate and voluntary activity.

Throughout the century, civil society grew. As citizen action flourished to address labor issues, civil rights, and social services, CSOs proliferated to unionize labor, advocate for civil rights, provide services to marginalized populations, protect the environment, and promote the general education, health, and development of society. This proliferation has been more pronounced in the last two decades of the century. Declining government fortunes and the end of the cold war have yielded opportunities, and often the necessity, for CSOs to develop where they had not previously enjoyed operating latitude or license.

One could argue that we experienced—and thankfully survived—experiments in monosector hegemony in the twentieth century. Perhaps the most important lesson from these experiments is that no sector is capable single-handedly of guiding society in ways that we believe are responsible and respectful in valuing the health, dignity, equity, and contribution of one and all. But even if we did indeed learn the lesson that no single sector is sufficient, we have yet to learn how to delegate roles, responsibilities, and resources among the different sectors effectively.

Corporate Citizenship at a Glance

While people still debate the definition of corporate citizenship, it is generally accepted to mean the practice of a corporation's direct responsibilities—to employees, shareholders, customers, suppliers, and to the communities where it conducts business and serves markets. Interpretations of what these "direct responsibilities" do or should entail vary widely. Forward-looking companies choose an interpretation that links responsibilities strategically with creating and maintaining a climate conducive to long-term business success. These companies also incorporate this interpretation in their philosophy, core values, and operations.

There has been important progress in advancing corporate citizenship since the mid-1980s.

- More companies around the world are openly addressing and enhancing their corporate citizenship practices. Many European, U.S., and Japanese companies have developed corporate citizenship strategies. For example, BP (British Petroleum) adopted a global framework for its community involvement, and is now working as BP-Amoco to integrate the strongest elements of the two companies' community programs worldwide. Levi Strauss and Co. has been recognized as an innovator in corporate citizenship, particularly through sourcing and supplier relationships and decisions and through direct support for important human resource issues (for example, AIDS, diversity). Similar strategies related to core business processes are being adopted by companies such as Nike, Starbucks, and Body Shop. Hitachi, Ltd. established a U.S. foundation and developed community involvement programs in North America, Europe, and Southeast Asia as its business and foreign direct investment in these regions grew.
- More companies are implementing deliberate corporate citizenship programs throughout their global operations, not solely in the communities and countries where headquarters are located.
- More companies are thinking about corporate citizenship strategically, integrating objectives across all functions of the business, knowing that these practices will be important in their long-term business success.

"Discussions of corporate citizenship and corporate engagement to strengthen civil society become most exciting when we focus on how companies earn and reinvest their revenues and how their expertise can be engaged in the larger task of societal development."

After all, business success depends on healthy, able workers; consumers with purchasing power; raw materials; and stable, predictable operating environments.

What can CSOs do to assist corporations in fulfilling needed roles? What challenges do CSOs and corporations face in forging these relationships?

While companies are taking their citizenship responsibilities more seriously, governments and community organizations are also working to advance corporate citizenship practices. Global communications have allowed communities and CSOs to publicize deleterious corporate practices and to mobilize opposition such as boycotts. Ignominy, or the fear thereof, has prompted many companies to "clean up their act," or it will have that effect in the not-too-distant future. It was once common, and even desirable, for companies to lower production standards in countries with less regulation, largely for cost savings, but this strategy will not be viable much longer. Both customers and communities can and do compare notes, and they increasingly demand consistent practices throughout a company's holdings and operations.

More companies and communities are demanding that suppliers also meet higher standards. Labor unions continue to push for improved working conditions and policies. In addition, CSOs are embracing the issue of corporate citizenship as their cause, and are engaging companies as members and service targets. These CSOs are developing strategies, tools, learning opportunities, and partnerships to advance and expand corporate citizenship practice. These actions are intended to influence how firms make what many refer to as "externalities" matters of internal corporate interest and investment.

Competition and peer influence also serve to advance corporate citizenship because favorable practices yield a competitive advantage. When differences in price, quality, and availability of products and services are negligible, sales and deals are often made on the basis of corporate citizenship practices. Consumers and shareholders increasingly scrutinize and favor companies with solid citizenship practices globally. Such activism was potent in overturning apartheid in South Africa. The socially responsible investment industry has grown dramatically, and it is delivering solid financial returns.

How Much Is Enough?

Despite the fact that there has been substantial progress globally in getting companies to enhance their corporate citizenship practices, most people worldwide do not think companies are doing nearly enough, or at least not in the ways we might want.

Companies first and foremost have to be profitable to be of any value to society. Healthy, profitable companies contribute to the community economically through the wages they pay workers, dividends they pay shareholders, taxes they pay governments, and contributions (monetary or other kinds of resources) or investments they make in community organizations and civic infrastructure. They can also contribute to the health and vitality of communities through their products, services, employment practices, and sourcing decisions. In thinking about engaging companies in strengthening civil society, we must bear in mind that companies inevitably and responsibly make bottom-line profitability their priority, and by so doing they contribute positively to society when they pay taxes and employee wages.

Beyond these actions, companies worldwide have pursued citizenship in many ways. In the United States, many companies and the general public think of corporate citizenship largely as charity, philanthropy, or "giving back to the community." The legal and regulatory system offers tax deductions when companies make charitable contributions. A relatively sophisticated system of corporate philanthropy has evolved. Still, there is a growing concern about the results—what is actually achieved, and whether there is any impact within communities or within the firm.

Bottom-line pressure is prompting many companies to undertake more strategic approaches and to link philanthropy or any other corporate giving to direct business interests. Managers are called on to assess the impact of philanthropic giving in terms of bottom-line results.

CSOs in the United States view these developments optimistically, cautiously, and even cynically too. There is discernible discomfort with the notion of strategic social investment that serves business self-interest even though it may simultaneously serve public interest. Yet, more companies and CSOs are exploring strategic approaches.

In Europe governments traditionally played an intermediary role between business and CSOs. Government collected taxes from firms, and subsequently distributed funds to CSOs in contracts and fees for specific services. Nonetheless, as the European Union has evolved and firms have globalized, practices that serve business and community interests simultaneously have been adopted, with growing direct interaction between firms and CSOs. While attitudes vary, there seems to be a higher level of public acceptance in European countries than in the United States for corporate community involvement to serve direct business interests.

In many Asian countries, and indeed throughout the world, there is often the sentiment that philanthropy is for individuals, not companies. Those holding this view stress that it is irresponsible to "give away" shareholders' money. Their argument maintains that we should instead expect those who succeed in business to become philanthropic as individuals.

Developing countries boast many of both the most traditional and most progressive corporate citizenship practices. Often companies have to build basic infrastructure simply to ensure their productive capacity: they build roads to access raw materials and transport finished products, they build health clinics and schools to ensure a supply of able workers, and they create supplier businesses to provide needed services. There are many examples of cross-sector collaboration in developing countries. In some countries companies, government, and CSOs have found strategic ways of working together. Still, such practice remains the exception worldwide rather than the norm.

Varying legal and regulatory frameworks, cultural norms, and public expectations yield vastly differing attitudes toward and practices in corporate citizenship. In the next millennium, civil society stands to gain far more from the strategic engagement of the private sector as partners in development than from mere charity. Creativity and resourcefulness in forging cross-sector partnerships and strategic alliance holds promise for companies and civil society alike.

Analysis and Observations

What do we need from companies, and how are we likely to get it? Proscribing corporate citizenship practice can only bring stale, one-size-fits-all, static actions, though it may establish standards for minimally acceptable conduct. Instead, we need companies to bring the same innovation, focus, and initiative to their citizenship that they bring to their business pursuits. We also need companies to integrate their citizenship actions throughout their operations. If the actions of a firm's R&D, product development, production, marketing, and sales divisions consistently promote human rights, for example, communities throughout the world benefit more extensively than they would from one or a few charitable contributions. We should not wish to see companies implementing their corporate citizenship solely through their philanthropic activities. By the same token, a company's philanthropic activities can and should provide guidance for how the company can invest strategically to build stronger communities, thereby establishing conditions for long-term business success.

Discussions of corporate citizenship and corporate engagement to strengthen civil society become most exciting when we focus on how companies earn and reinvest their revenues and how their expertise can be engaged in the larger task of societal development. It is through core business decisions, operations, and expertise that we can mobilize and leverage corporate resources most effectively in strengthening communities and society.

Why should we engage business in building and strengthening civil society?

- Engage corporate resources (financial, human, technical, network) in addressing social and environmental issues.
- Influence business culture and operations to make them ever more responsible and productive socially and environmentally.
- Build employee capacity to participate in strengthening civil society through corporate actions and through their individual participation as citizens, with CSOs and in public life generally.

To be successful, companies need public acceptance and goodwill. They need investors, workers, raw materials, markets, and consumers. They also need predictable operating environments. Civil society can help provide all of these necessary ingredients and in turn can benefit from the expertise and resources that companies have to offer in exchange.

Engage Corporate Resources

Engaging companies means thinking creatively about the full range of resources they bring to the table. A basic, though not complete list of these resources includes companies' employees; their intellectual assets, such as their innovations, creativity, and specific areas of expertise; their work processes and facilities; their products and services; their networks of suppliers, customers, shareholders, and industry counterparts; and their profits.

Corporate philanthropy and giving programs are typically "back end" programs. They occur at the end of the production process when there are profits available for such activities. Even the funding streams attest to this "end of the pipeline" mentality, because many corporate programs are supported through receiving a set portion of the previous year's after-tax profits. As back end actions, they have not had to be as strategic or creative because they are simply intended to give something back to the community and promote a positive image of the company. We now face the exciting prospect of integrating corporate citizenship objectives at each stage of corporate activity, and it is reasonable to expect returns on the investments both within the firm and in the target communities.

> *"More companies are thinking about corporate citizenship strategically, integrating objectives across all functions of the business, knowing that these practices will be important in their long-term business success."*

If companies and communities adopt more of a research and development attitude toward philanthropy, corporate giving, corporate community involvement, and partnerships, the possibilities are vast. This kind of ethic would place a premium on learning from program experiences. It would be more "patient" in anticipating results, meaning that longer gestation periods would be granted. It would prompt close alliances with and partnerships among CSO and corporate venture partners, who would interact to develop approaches or products, in some cases commercializing and in other cases simply disseminating the results.

For example, if a global communications firm has recruitment and community involvement programs with CSOs that address minority or special populations (for example, sight-impaired), the firm has access to networks and information (for example, language, culture, use patterns, and preferences) that are relevant, and potentially valuable, to future products, markets, and workers. When Kodak observed the antiapartheid boycott and left South Africa, its main rival, Fuji Film, became the dominant player in the market. When Kodak returned, regaining its previous market share presented a huge challenge. Ultimately, it had to broaden the market: the townships became a marketing target. The company realized that new film products were needed, ones made to capture darker skin tones more effectively. Community involvement strategies in these townships and in other places where people have darker skin tones could have provided the impetus, networks, and technical information that might have brought such product innovations and market opportunities sooner. One can only speculate as to whether substantial CSO-corporate relationships in the townships, in support of education or human services for example, might have helped end apartheid sooner.

In these cases, if corporate community involvement strategies were pursued, the communities and CSOs would benefit from access to resources, new networks, and relationships. The key to making such links productive for communities and companies is for the relationships to be genuine and ethical, built on mutual benefit and respect, and for there to be channels for moving the experience and insights constructively through the respective institutions.

Considerations addressed in corporate R&D more easily find expression throughout corporate operations. If, for example, use of services by many cultural groups is not considered in the early stages of development, chances are the services will not be designed as appropriately for multicultural use and marketing and advertising will not target these groups.

The key here is to pursue CSO-corporate relationships that help all parties see the opportunities for working together at different stages of their work. CSOs are often at the cutting edge of societal research, development, and change. They see issues in the earliest stages of development and design programs to address them. Think of the learning and innovation possible if the diagnostic and preventative strategies CSOs undertake were supported with a broad range of corporate resources, including communications. Many kinds of CSO-corporate relationships are possible. Adversarial relations are at one end of a continuum of the range of possible interaction, and true collaboration and partnerships are at the other end. Selection of the most appropriate actions and relationships is an important consideration. In the past we have probably relied too heavily on adversarial relations and have not invested enough time or attention in building partnerships.

Influence Business Culture and Operations

Civil society can influence business culture and operations through partnerships as well as through a range of other activities. For example, World Resources Institute worked with several firms to identify the full range of the firms' environmental costs. Once the costs were visible to managers and executives, they made decisions about production processes that were more environmentally benign. They based decisions on sound business logic, but civil society benefited too. In some cases, highly toxic production processes were curbed or eliminated completely, with corresponding improvements in environmental protection.

Prospects for influencing business culture and operations are particularly strong regarding the environment, workforce issues, investment strategies and policies, and corporate transitions such as downsizing. Now that firms are global, employees worldwide increasingly expect consistent employment policies and benefits. CSOs can play valuable roles in helping to craft effective policies and in adapting these to differing cultural circumstances.

Perhaps there are no more powerful ways to influence business culture and operations than through shareholder and consumer activism. Because companies have to focus on their bottom-line profitability, both in the short and long term, the financial leverage held by investors and consumers is broad and deep. If investors and consumers increasingly choose investments or products based on corporate citizenship considerations, other companies will take on these objectives and activities just to compete. Alternately, if investors and consumers deliberately avoid certain companies because of their practices, these companies will not long survive.

Build Employee Capacity

What roles must citizens play in forging mutually beneficial relations between companies and CSOs? Employees influence business culture and operations. Employees also play many other community roles: parents, citizens, volunteers, elected officials, mentors, tutors, and role models. If we develop programs and partnerships that enhance their capacity, there are benefits on the job and in the many other activities they undertake. Companies can exercise their citizenship largely through how they treat employees and how they build employees' capacities. At the same time, companies can contribute extensively to the communities by supporting their employees to be involved in addressing and resolving community issues. This is a leadership challenge for companies and communities. For example, providing health care and educational services to employees has broad ripple effects within communities. By the same token, making sure that employees have reasonable working hours and encouraging their involvement in community action allows them to share their expertise and skills as CSO volunteers and board members.

So What?

There is a far greater potential return in engaging companies to contribute from their core competencies than is likely from proscribing or unnecessarily limiting their involvement or by ignoring or excluding companies from important discussions on civil society. After all, corporate actions are prominent in driving the changes transforming our world. Our responses to these changes must likewise engage companies or they are likely to fail. We must also develop the capacity to influence the direction of the changes and of corporate behavior.

The same mandate for engaging corporations in strengthening civil society applies to CSOs and to the voluntary/nonprofit sector generally. We must engage the full range of resources and resourcefulness available within the sector, we must influence CSO culture and operations positively, and we must build employee capacity.

CSOs and companies must use the full range of tools at their disposal to craft the most effective standards and practices of corporate citizenship. Legislation and regulation can provide important tools and boundaries that eliminate deleterious practice. At the same time, there must be incentives for constantly improving practice. There must be room for creativity, innovation, and experimentation. There also has to be acknowledgment of promising and good practices, particularly those that are sustainable, even if they are modest in magnitude.

Promoting corporate-CSO interaction of many kinds will shed light on what tools are most effective in what circumstances. For example, when is corporate philanthropy the most effective tool, and for what purposes; when is affiliation with collective actions most effective; when are partnerships and collaboration most effective; and when does in-kind giving make the most sense for the firm and for the community?

Increased CSO-corporate interaction will also yield better tools with which we can understand the impact of actions within both companies and communities. If we only measure how a company's community actions affect its bottom line, we miss an important opportunity for strengthening civil society. If we can instead develop tools that more accurately assess community impact while also conveying bottom-line relevance, we can encourage more promising, effective practice among companies. It is critical that we understand impact comprehensively, rather than in one or two dimensions.

Firms can integrate corporate citizenship objectives throughout their operations in ways that improve profits and communities. Corporate-CSO partnerships are key to realizing such potential.

RECOMMENDATIONS

Ultimately, we want corporations to engage in strengthening civil society in three important ways:

- strategic business interest
- business-community partnerships
- corporate philanthropy

Building Blocks for Corporate Engagement

All of these strategies require independent action and effective partners. To promote the kinds of independent action and collaboration we need from corporations and CSOs, several fundamental habits and strategies are essential.

Understand identity, values, and mission—CSOs and companies must know themselves before they can collaborate effectively. This self-knowledge helps determine the most appropriate kinds of partnerships and opportunities for collaboration. It also helps organizations avoid disastrous relationships.

Think strategically—CSOs and companies have the most to gain from win-win opportunities where there are tangible benefits for all parties.

Do research—Proper research and investigation identify appropriate potential corporate and CSO partners and activities. Research also helps partners know one another and develop means of working together.

Identify self-interest and common interest—Partnerships must meet the needs of the respective partners. Knowing what parties need and why they want to participate leads to program designs that satisfy these needs.

Consider the broad range of resources that exist—Companies contribute most effectively through their core competencies. They cannot, and will not, write blank checks—even if they had the funds, it would not be in their interest, or the community's, to contribute to society primarily in this way. Likewise, CSOs have a range of resources that they need to understand, publicize, and use strategically and effectively. Their experience, analysis, constituents, and networks prepare them to bring intellectual capital and implementing ability into partnerships.

Identify supportive partners and networks—Even the most effective partnership cannot solve all of the challenges civil society addresses. One goal should always be to link up with networks that can help assess, disseminate, and advance the work and results of a single partnership or collective actions.

Communicate, educate, and inform—Cross-sector partnerships can foster learning. For example, companies can benefit from the knowledge CSOs have on the societal issues around which engagement is sought. CSOs can benefit from the managerial and technical knowledge that companies have. The only way to overcome the stereotypes and preconceived notions that each sector holds about the other sectors is to invest in communication, education, and information that helps the parties transcend their preconceptions and collaborate effectively. Communicating about the art, science, practice, and products of partnership is equally important.

Respect and learn from cultural differences—As we promote corporate-CSO partnerships globally, we confront myriad challenges that stem from cultural differences, whether the "cultural" differences are sectoral, organizational, or ethnic. Cross-cultural relationships are difficult. They require knowledge, awareness, sensitivity, and skills that all too few have acquired. Just as being literate helps people navigate the world of communication, we need to develop ways of being "culturate" to navigate this world of many cultures adeptly, responsibly, and respectfully.

Be realistic and start small—Building corporate-CSO relationships in support of civil society takes time and practice. Developing effective relationships means that parties establish ways of working together to dream, think, plan, act, troubleshoot, resolve differences, evaluate, and learn. It is as important to develop means for resolving conflicts jointly as it is to agree on how to communicate program results. All parties need to be able and willing to listen, negotiate, compromise, and deliver high standards of conduct.

Evaluate and learn from the partnership and activities—The true test of partnership is whether the partners change as a result of their interaction. Advocating effective corporate-CSO partnerships necessarily means that we are seeking change within firms, within CSOs, and within communities. It is important for the parties to work jointly to identify what impact they are trying to achieve and to develop the tools for assessing what impact they actually have—intended and unanticipated. A great deal of the work civil society undertakes has a long gestation period. Results may take many years to deliver. One challenge in developing appropriate evaluation and learning strategies is to identify shorter-term indicators that help partners know they are on the road to success.

Take risks—Take risks, but draw on past experience and available data to ensure the risks are intelligent, or at least studied and deliberately accepted. Firms and CSOs alike need to take risks to move the practice of corporate citizenship forward in ways that offer benefits for communities, CSOs, and firms.

Advancing Corporate Citizenship in the Next Millennium

In the future, engaging corporations effectively in strengthening civil society will require attention to several issues. These areas are ripe for further exploration and advancement.

Identifying Promising Practice—The so-called "watch dog" CSOs highlight deleterious corporate behavior, but there is far less highlighting of practices we do want companies to adopt. We need material that helps firms know what promising practices look like, how they are implemented, and how much (or little) they cost. We need information in many formats (print, electronic, multimedia, training courses) providing examples, case studies, research, and analysis of good and promising practices. CSOs, even the watch dog CSOs, are well positioned to assist in this important task.

Developing Incentive Systems—We need meaningful incentive systems that reward the kinds of conduct we most want and that acknowledge progress. Likewise, we need disincentives for behaviors we want to eliminate. Shareholder activism, consumer activism, and competitive advantage will help provide understandable incentives for favorable corporate citizenship. CSOs have a role to play. They must help craft incentive systems that serve compa-

"If investors and consumers increasingly choose investments or products based on corporate citizenship considerations, other companies will take on these objectives and activities just to compete. Alternately, if investors and consumers deliberately avoid certain companies because of their practices, these companies will not long survive."

nies, communities, and CSOs effectively. They must also assist in responsible shareholder and consumer activism.

Understanding the Art, Science, and Limitations of Partnerships—In the late 1990s partnership became the mandate, at least rhetorically. Everyone now talks about partnerships, but few are actually working in them. True partnerships exist only when risks, decisions, and rewards are shared. Because true corporate-CSO partnerships are rare, we need to elicit, document, and analyze all possible learning from those that do exist. We also need to know more about when, and under what circumstances, partnerships are an effective strategy and when they are not.

Practicing Collaboration—Collaboration is easier said than done. We need incentives, training, support, and practice to learn how to collaborate effectively. It is difficult enough when those trying to collaborate come from similar cultural backgrounds. It is far more difficult when we complicate the situation with cultural differences, whether institutional or ethnic, but it is also more rewarding. Collaboration will only become easier when we better understand factors of success and after we get lots of practice.

Designing Appropriate Measurement and Assessment Tools—Companies worldwide want to measure the results of their citizenship activities more effectively. Measurement projects are helping companies relate results to the bottom line, but few are helping firms understand impact within both the company and the community. The period of investigation is often too short for accurate evaluation. Firms and CSOs must work together to develop more effective tools to assess civil society work. CSO practitioners, program participants, and corporate employees need flexible tools to monitor results and provide feedback for program improvement, revamping, or elimination, as appropriate.

Creating Monitoring and Enforcement Strategies—Advanced communications technologies facilitate monitoring of corporate and CSO behavior. Still, there are too few tools for enforcement. Community organizing is one strategy but with limitations—it is often more crisis oriented than preventative. International standards may prove increasingly helpful if they are developed around a broader range of corporate citizenship indicators. After all, firms already adhere to environmentally oriented **International Organization for Standardization** (ISO) standards, and they strive to meet many other ISO standards to be competitive globally. We may need global organizations that assist in monitoring and enforcing functions, or we may simply need better incentive and disincentive systems that make the market function in support of civil society and community problem solving.

Making Use of Established Practices and Networks—Corporate citizenship activities are easiest to implement when they are integrated in things people and companies already do. This means that programming needs to occur within a firm's daily routine. Programming also needs to occur and be reinforced in the firm's established networks, whether these are customer or supplier chains, local chambers of commerce, industry associations, or national and global networks organized around business interests.

Institutionalizing Relationships—Companies and CSOs need to explore how and when it makes sense to institutionalize relationships so they are less vulnerable to personnel turnover. Existing corporate-CSO partnerships are often based on personal relationships between two or a few people, and relationships end if these critical few leave or change responsibilities. Long-term relationships only make sense when all parties add value. The value companies and CSOs bring to the table must be communicated to and draw upon ever-expanding sets of players within partner institutions to ensure that relationships do not end solely because one or two people change positions.

Building Forums for Cross-Sector Interaction and Problem Solving—With increasing specialization globally, forums where the different sectors of society interact are becoming rare. In the few that do exist, behavior is often proscribed or conditioned to prevent change. If we are to achieve a sensible division of labor among the government, private for-profit, and nonprofit/voluntary sectors, we need forums where these sectors can and do interact regularly and purposefully. We need forums at all levels of organization: local, national, regional, and global.

Responding and Adapting to Ever-changing Circumstances—The pace of change in the twentieth century shows no sign of slowing. Companies, CSOs, and governments will all need to be agile and strategic to survive in the next millennium. They will need to be skilled in the art of interdependence and skilled in embracing diversity. Perhaps the single most important set of skills will relate to how individuals and institutions make decisions about what to keep and what to shed in the continuous remodeling (or reinventions) of organization that are likely in the face of future change. What will be the core values, commitments, and practices that we sustain?

"Perhaps there are no more powerful ways to influence business culture and operations than through shareholder and consumer activism."

Contributing to Peace, Security, and Stability—Throughout the twentieth century governments used resource flows as tools of domestic and foreign policy to promote stability (or to foster instability). Private investment flows now dwarf overseas development assistance. This fact places the private sector squarely in the peace, security, and stability business, whether by choice or default. Though an individual company might not tip the balance, capital markets and collective private sector behavior profoundly affect stability within countries. In the 1990s we had several examples of the destabilizing effects of international capital markets. The private sector must act deliberately to support peace, security, and stability—it is in the direct interest of businesses to do so.

Thinking of Corporate Citizenship as R&D and as Fundamental to Business Success—Business and communities can both win if firms consider the societal context and critical issues as integral to the R&D of their businesses in the short and long term. Corporate R&D seeks to anticipate and develop future opportunities. Corporate citizenship has the same fundamental purpose. Partnerships with CSOs to address poverty alleviation or AIDS research are typically described in current terms: they address current critical problems. But they actually anticipate potential future costs and future labor markets. Focusing on the current is not bad, it is simply insufficient. When companies and CSOs think about how their work, independently and jointly, delivers both current and future returns, it may be easier to justify and support. Dedicated support usually delivers substantially higher returns than intermittent support.

Thinking of Business Involvement as Fundamental to Civil Society Success—Involving business—its operations and its employees—in civil society is fundamental to civil society's ability to achieve its potential. Companies provide indirect (through taxes and through employee salaries, which correspondingly yield taxes and charitable contributions) and direct financial support to civil society. Perhaps because business involvement has often been perceived in only these limited ways, we do not appreciate business' broader, more fundamental involvement in civil society. For example, corporate employees are part of the public, acting within and through civil society as interested citizens. Civil society is stronger when it engages the business sector in its efforts.

Closing Thoughts

Many current initiatives offer the prospect of important insights about corporate citizenship and corporate-CSO partnerships. Advancements, and possibly real breakthroughs, are likely to emerge from these and similar efforts. A few examples of such initiatives include:

- Business Partners in Development, a collaboration of the World Bank, global companies, and global CSOs such as the Prince of Wales Business Leaders Forum and CIVICUS;
- The Hitachi Foundation's Corporate Volunteerism Initiative, evaluated by the Boston College Center for Corporate Community Relations;
- The Japan Center for International Exchange's project to study corporate-community partnerships in the Asia Pacific region;
- CIVICUS's Corporate Engagement Initiative;
- The European Business Network for Social Cohesion;
- EMPRESA—The Forum on Business and Social Responsibility in the Americas; and
- The World Business Council for Sustainable Development.

A growing number of institutions are promoting and facilitating corporate citizenship through membership programming. Examples of these organizations include Business for Social Responsibility, Philippine Business for Social Progress, and AIESEC International.

Companies and CSOs are also important to watch in the next millennium because they are agents of organizational and institutional change. Many are supranational and are developing organizational practices and institutional forms that reflect and draw on their global presence. This global presence represents valuable capacity and opportunity for addressing the most vexing issues society faces—globally and locally.

Achieving a healthy global society requires that corporate, civil society, and government actors find appropriate ways to interact, collaborate, and exercise their respective independent roles. As we try to adjust to our radically changing global community, while striving to maintain the creativity, diversity, and integrity of the world's people and environment, the corporate sector can be a strong ally. The business sector will only be a strong ally if we work to engage companies substantively and deliberately in building and strengthening civil society. The kinds of tools we need to be skilled in using to advance broad-scale development in our societies range from collaborative to adversarial: for example, partnerships and collaboration, contracts, regulation, boycotts, media coverage, organizing, citizen action, incentive systems, employee volunteerism, award programs, codes of conduct, standards, grants and contributions, purchasing power, investment decisions, and program related investments.

We will only accomplish constructive business engagement with civil society if we—business and civil society—use all available tools strategically, creatively, and effectively. We also need to develop new tools that enhance the ability of companies, CSOs, and governments to communicate and work together effectively to serve the interests of all humanity as creatively, adequately, and equitably as possible.

Laurie Regelbrugge joined CIVICUS as chief operating officer and general manager in May 1999. Before that she was vice president of The Hitachi Foundation, a U.S. philanthropic organization established in 1985 by Hitachi, Ltd. of Tokyo, Japan, where she managed a U.S.$3 million annual grantmaking program supporting U.S. nonprofit organizations in education, community development, and global citizenship projects. She also managed partnership programs with Hitachi companies through which local community action strategies were developed and implemented by employee teams. Before joining the Foundation in 1990, Ms. Regelbrugge worked in several nonprofit organizations, directing domestic and international programs in education, community and economic development, and management. She is a coauthor of Global Corporate Citizenship: Rationale and Strategies *and is a frequent speaker and writer on the subjects of corporate citizenship, community development, collaboration, and multicultural education.*

Mapping Corporate Citizenship: A Survey of Global, National, and Local Initiatives

3

Maxwell Brem, under the direction of Christopher Pinney

INTRODUCTION

This chapter surveys the corporate citizenship field on a global basis. It describes the main players in this field, identifies the significant organizations and programs currently promoting corporate citizenship and corporate engagement with civil society around the world, and describes some of the national, regional, and international initiatives that are under way.

It is worth noting that the majority of these programs and organizations were established within the last five years—many of them within the last two. Thus their mandates and operations are still evolving. Where possible we have tried to indicate the scope of their achievements, as well as describing their mandates and goals.

This inventory has been taken from a number of sources, including profiles supplied by the organizations themselves, information supplied by members of the CIVICUS Corporate Engagement Task Force, and research by Imagine, a program of the Canadian Centre for Philanthropy. It is not intended to be an exhaustive list. It represents the majority of players in the area of corporate citizenship, but in such a growing field, new organizations, and branches of existing organizations, will continue to appear. The information below has been drawn from available material and is intended to give an overview of each initiative but is not comprehensive. More detailed information can be obtained from the organizations concerned. It is important to note that we have relied on information given and that we have not been able to check the actual performance of many of the initiatives the research has uncovered. Nonetheless, the data gathered for this survey of the global landscape combine to make an impressive statement about the development and growth of corporate citizenship initiatives. We would welcome information about any significant organizations that have been omitted.

It has been necessary to develop a preliminary classification for the purpose of grouping the wide variety of programs, networks, and organizations that are working to encourage and assist companies to become better corporate citizens. No classification is perfect, since the functions and mandates of some organizations overlap among categories. The following are the classifications used in the paper:

- "Intermediate" groups and networks working to expand corporate citizenship—at global, regional, and national levels;
- Corporate participation in policy dialogue on social and other issues that affect civil society;
- Multilateral programs that promote corporate citizenship and corporate engagement;
- Membership-based, capacity-building business organizations with a focus on developing corporate social responsibility and citizenship;
- Research and teaching institutions that specialize in corporate citizenship and related issues;
- Selected private consultancies supporting leadership initiatives in corporate engagement; and
- Selected other organizations.

"INTERMEDIATE" GROUPS AND NETWORKS WORKING TO EXPAND CORPORATE CITIZENSHIP

A new type of organizational entity has made its appearance in recent years expressly for the purpose of fostering business engagement with civil society and its concerns. These entities have sprung up at international, regional, national, and local-urban levels. Composed of networks of leaders of business and civil society, these "intermediate" groups—sometimes also called "intermediary organizations"—promote a range of relationships between the two sectors and interact to facilitate cross-sectoral partnerships. In some countries public sector agencies may be involved as well.

These bodies act as catalysts for a new style of collaboration and a new way of addressing responsibilities at the end of the twentieth century. With their concentrated focus on exploring opportunities, the education of business leaders, partnership development, and dissemination of best practices, intermediate entities set out to attract new adherents to corporate citizenship. Many start off as offshoots, or semi-autonomous programs, of existing organizations. New ones are appearing each year.

Operating as change agents, the networks that form around the new entities mobilize the private sector to become involved in the social agenda. They are, in addition, a channel for technical assistance and other resources to support the development of business-community partnerships and community investment programs. Other roles include representation to government with a view to creating a more favorable tax and "enabling" environment for corporate citizenship. Where the private sector is being asked to play a more direct role in advancing social and economic development, such as in the former Communist countries, the intermediate entities often provide a forum for discussing the private sector's contribution in conjunction with civil society groups. In some countries, programs have resulted that are closely supportive of national development goals.

In their structure, composition, and values, these entities contain elements of a new, genuinely "hybrid" model of nonprofit organization. Civic-minded business leaders, frequently linked to multinational firms, often provide the dynamic leadership of "intermediates," and much of the organizational and program funding comes from business sources. But the work is developed in close conjunction with key leaders from civil society, who also provide the driving initiative. Organizational values may reflect both civil society goals and the long-term strategic interests of business, especially large businesses planning a long-term presence in a country.

In many parts of the world, a core group of multinational companies appear to provide the leadership and money for a number of the "intermediate" initiatives. By active participation and by being champions of community involvement and corporate citizenship, global firms set a clear example. The size and influence of multinationals enables them to recruit additional firms to the corporate citizenship standard—both large nationally based firms and fellow multinationals. Of course, there are advantages in being seen as a leader. The activist firms stand to gain "brownie points" with government, regulatory, and civic authorities, and this can be particularly useful to a firm when it is entering or wanting to expand in a new market. In a more direct sense, participation in leadership networks with civil society representatives can help global firms to identify local partners and better understand the circumstances of the country and the opportunities for civic engagement.

Global Initiatives

The Prince of Wales Business Leaders Forum

The leading example of an "intermediate" initiative at the global level is **The Prince of Wales Business Leaders Forum (PWBLF)**, headquartered in the U.K.

Established in 1990, The Prince of Wales Business Leaders Forum is a global network of business leaders from Europe, North and South America, Africa, the Middle East, and the Asia Pacific region. Established in Britain as an outgrowth of a national initiative (Business in the Community, described below), it has two primary goals. The first goal is to raise awareness of the value of corporate responsibility both to the successful management of international business and to the prosperity of the host countries and communities. The second goal is to encourage partnership action between business, government, communities, civil society organizations (CSOs), and aid agencies, as an effective means of promoting sustainable development. It achieves these goals through a strategy of:

- Advocacy—researching and communicating good practice of business-led partnerships in social and economic development;
- Brokerage—acting as a catalyst to bring together organizations from different sectors to work on specific joint projects;
- Capacity and institution building—running workshops and training programs.

The Forum's mission "is to promote socially responsible business practices that benefit business and society and which help to achieve social, economic and environmentally sustainable development. . . . The Forum is successful when it encourages business to maximise the positive and minimise the negative impact of their operations."

The Forum works with its member companies and local affiliated organizations in seventeen developing and transition countries. It also has strategic alliances with a small number of international development agencies and an International Partnership Network of over five hundred "partnership practitioners" drawn from business, CSOs, community-based organizations (CBOs), the media, academia, development agencies, and government. It runs the International Hotels Environment Initiative, supported by leading hotel chains and hotel associations around the world. Programs that have proven to be successful in the U.K. or other countries are often adapted to local circumstances.

PWBLF defines cross-sector partnerships as a coming together of representatives of business, civil society, and the public sector (or two of the three) in a relationship designed to fulfill a particular purpose or task. The partnership will have agreed expectations and commitments, and risks and benefits will be shared.

As noted above, PWBLF has helped establish national forums in countries such as Poland, Hungary, and China. Indeed, much of the intellectual leadership for current developments in the thinking and practice of corporate

> ***Examples of Global Initiatives***
> - The Prince of Wales Business Leaders Forum: advocacy, brokerage, capacity and institution building
> - Business Partners for Development: trisector partnerships addressing international development projects

citizenship has come from the research and policy work of the PWBLF. In the past several years, this has emerged from its cooperative project with the **World Bank Group's** Finance and Private Sector Development Division and the UN Development Program. This global learning and networking initiative, known as **Business Partners for Development (BPD)**, seeks to identify, analyze, and promote examples of how business is working in partnership with public sector institutions, CSOs, and other private sector firms to play a creative and positive role in the process of sustainable development. Research for the project will include:

- An inventory of corporate good practice—drawn from different countries and industry sectors and covering a wide variety of business activities, and
- A detailed analysis of the policies and practices of twenty leading multinational companies from different sectors.

Key stakeholder groups will be surveyed for their perspectives on the changing role of business in society. This will involve surveys and interviews with local and national politicians, the media, CSOs, and CBOs, development professionals, business leaders, academics, and youths. (The World Bank-led and UNDP programs are discussed further in a later section.) CIVICUS is involved with the Prince of Wales Business Leaders Forum and the World Bank Group in BPD's Knowledge Resource Group.

Sectoral Initiatives

World Business Council for Sustainable Development

The **World Business Council for Sustainable Development (WBCSD)** is a coalition of more than a hundred and twenty business leaders drawn from thirty-four countries and more than twenty major industrial sectors. The council is linked to a network of national and regional business councils and partner organizations involving another six hundred companies, many of them leaders in their industries. The council's objectives are:

- To be the leading business advocate on issues connected with the environment and sustainable development;
- To participate in policy development to create a framework that allows business to contribute effectively to sustainable development;
- To demonstrate progress in environmental and resource management in business and to share leading-edge practices among its members; and
- To contribute to a sustainable future for developing nations and nations in transition.

A WBCSD working group is seeking to define what companies should do to respond to the challenge of corporate social responsibility (CSR) with regard to sustainable development, and what companies have already done to meet this challenge. It is also sponsoring dialogues with various international stakeholders. In 1998 working group members established a common working definition of corporate social responsibility and began to collect codes, principles, and other such documents used by their leading corporate members and to analyze them for commonalities. This analysis is being used to broadly describe the issues and core values that best define what CSR strives to comprehend.

The CSR action team formed by the working group reached the following provisional definition of CSR at a meeting in London in January 1998: "Corporate Social Responsibility is the sustainable commitment by business to contribute to development and to the well-being and the improvement of the quality of life of employees, their families and the community at large."

Global Business Council on HIV/AIDS

In 1997 a group of leading multinational companies came together with the Geneva-based UNAIDS organization to form the Global Business Council on HIV/AIDS. This "virtual" organization aims to share good practice on the different ways in which business can tackle HIV/AIDS both in the workplace and in partnership with customers, governments, and communities.

It should be noted that neither WBCSD nor the Global Council on HIV/AIDS can yet be described as an effective intermediary providing leadership for business in terms of the full roles described above. However, both have potential to move in that direction.

Examples of Sectoral Initiatives

- World Business Council for Sustainable Development: business advocacy, policy development, and demonstration on issues of the environment and sustainable development
- Global Business Council on HIV/AIDS: promote good practice on business efforts to address HIV/AIDS effectively

Regional Initiatives

European Foundation Centre—Corporate Citizenship Europe

At the regional level the Brussels-based **European Foundation Centre (EFC)** has created several major initiatives to build relations between the corporate and voluntary sectors.

Corporate Citizenship Europe (CCE) is a committee representing mostly trans-European companies that are corporate or foundation members of the European Foundation Centre. The individuals involved in the committee are drawn primarily from community and public affairs departments in the member organizations that are dedicated to strengthening communities in Europe.

Corporate Citizenship Europe operates two programs: the Intermediaries Interest Group and the Action Program to Promote Corporate Giving.

- Intermediaries Interest Group. Recognizing the role that intermediates can play in building support for corporate citizenship across European frontiers, this group aims to strengthen independent organizations to act as intermediaries and to build effective bridges between corporate citizenship programs and the civil society sector in Europe. This is essentially a capacity-building initiative.
- Action Program to Promote Corporate Giving. This initiative aims to deepen the commitment to corporate giving among companies that are expanding their operations in Europe. Here the target companies include both European-origin firms and multinationals originating outside Europe. Meetings and research conducted under this second CCE program have focused on how corporate expansion programs can contribute optimally to improving the quality of life in the societies in which the operations are situated. In this sense, the work builds on existing achievements and the core work of the CCE committee and Intermediaries Interest Group to promote greater corporate responsibility in society. A

seminar in Italy in May 1996 illustrates the approach. It sought to direct corporate philanthropic attention away from traditional corporate giving to the arts, culture, and heritage and toward more pressing community needs.

The CCE Secretariat sponsors European-level conferences on corporate citizenship, study visits by senior executives, and benchmarking publications.

In addition, the European Foundation Centre's independently funded **Orpheus Program** provides a public record and information service on foundations and corporate citizenship programs in Europe.

The European Foundation Centre has spawned yet another, somewhat related, initiative, known as the **Trans-Atlantic Civil Society Dialogue Project (TACD)**. Projects conducted by a TACD working group include:

- Corporations in Society. This foresees the development of a database on successful European Union and U.S. corporate-funded projects and employee programs that have contributed toward strengthening civil society. It will include a study of senior corporate executives on their role as business leaders in society.
- Investment in the Community. This aims to develop models for locally based community investment and will feature local corporate citizens coming together with community foundations as partners in strengthening civil society and taking measures against social exclusion.
- Citizen-to-Citizen Links. This is aimed at involving ordinary citizens, including ethnic minorities who may now feel excluded, in trans-Atlantic exchanges using the Internet.

Established in 1989 by seven of Europe's leading foundations, the European Foundation Centre today has a membership of over a hundred and sixty independent funders and serves a further seven thousand organizations linked through networking centers in thirty-five countries worldwide.

European Business Network for Social Cohesion

The **European Business Network for Social Cohesion** originated when a group of leading business managers approved the *European Declaration of Business against Exclusion* in January 1995. It is an example of how companies have come together on a national and regional basis to work with other firms and with government to tackle problems of unemployment and social exclusion in the workplace. The network identifies and seeks to promote business-driven approaches to tackling five main issue-areas where companies can take action:

- promoting integration of the labor market;
- helping to improve vocational training;
- avoiding layoffs or providing alternatives where layoffs are inevitable;
- promoting the creation of new jobs and new businesses; and
- contributing to social integration in economically depressed areas and among particularly marginalized groups.

Some of Europe's most successful businesses are members of the network. They are supported by a range of enterprise and development agencies such as the London Enterprise Agency, the Dutch and German Federation of Christian Employers, Soldalitas, the King Baudouin Foundation, Uniapac, and others.

The European Bahá'í Business Forum

The **European Bahá'í Business Forum** (EBBF) is a global network of about three hundred men and women in business from forty-six countries. Although membership is global, activities are focused in Europe. EBBF is drawing increasing attention in Europe through its publications, its participation in United Nations summit conferences (including the recent World Business Forums in Istanbul and Stockholm), and its projects to promote entrepreneurship and ethics in many Eastern and Central European countries.

Asia Pacific Philanthropy Consortium

Formally launched in December 1994, the **Asia Pacific Philanthropy Consortium** (APPC) is a regionwide network that is dedicated to advancing the nonprofit sector's role in addressing social and economic needs in cooperation with governments and businesses.

The consortium seeks to promote the role of philanthropy in addressing critical issues in the Asia Pacific region; to increase the flow and effectiveness of philanthropic giving within and to the region; to respond to the institution-building needs of existing and emerging civil society and nonprofit organizations through networking, human resource development, and research; and to facilitate efforts by philanthropic organizations in the region to identify and collaborate in addressing issues of mutual concern.

Through its programs and conferences, APPC has emerged as the primary intermediate-level Asia region forum for discussion of corporate citizenship issues. Business partnership issues were prominently discussed at the International Conference on Supporting the Nonprofit Sector in Asia, convened by APPC in Bangkok in January 1998. Moreover, since the onset of the Asian financial crisis in 1997, the issue of corporate support for the civil society sector has become more critical. Incomes have fallen, millions of people have been plunged back into poverty, and government budget cutting has targeted social sector programs. The APPC is expected to play a greater role in fostering cross-sectoral partnership building and dialogue.

The APPC is led by a six-person executive committee from Australia, Korea, Japan, the Philippines, and the United States. "Lead agencies" within the region are responsible for specific programs organized under consortium auspices.

EMPRESA—Forum on Business and Social Responsibility in the Americas

The **EMPRESA** Forum is a new alliance of business organizations devoted to the promotion of corporate social responsibility in the Americas. Its founders are companies with annual revenues exceeding U.S.$1.5 trillion. The founding organizations include small, medium, and large domestic and international companies that operate in the commercial, service, industrial, and financial sectors.

EMPRESA came into being following a conference in the region sponsored by the U.S. organization **Business for Social Responsibility (BSR)** and financed through its Education Fund. EMPRESA's mission is to foster national and regional business organizations that promote social and environmental responsibility as a core corporate value. It will facilitate the growth of a Latin American network through collaboration, information exchange, education, applied research, networking, and partnerships among the constituent groups and their members. Currently, EMPRESA in conjunction with BSR is supporting the creation of organizational structures to promote socially responsible business and corporate engagement in several Latin American countries.

National Initiatives

A wide range of national level intermediate initiatives is described below. The features of the initiatives invariably reflect the characteristics of each country as well as the level of development and experience with corporate citizenship.

Argentina

Following the creation of EMPRESA cited above, leaders of eleven major enterprises in Buenos Aires endorsed the founding of **Business for Social Responsibility—Argentina (la Asociacion de Empresarios por la Responsabilidad Social)**. The objective is to promote corporate citizenship in five areas: the environment, workplace, community, the markets, and human rights.

Examples of Regional Initiatives

- European Foundation Centre Corporate Citizenship Europe
- European Business Network for Social Cohesion
- The European Bahá'í Business Forum
- Asia Pacific Philanthropy Consortium
- EMPRESA—Forum on Business and Social Responsibility in the Americas

Australia

Philanthropy Australia, the umbrella body for major grantmaking private, family, and corporate trusts and foundations in Australia, is currently developing its corporate engagement program. As a result of the round table conference convened by the Australian prime minister in March 1998, an awards program has been established to recognize partnerships between business and community organizations operating in Australia. The first awards were given out in 1998.

Brazil

Created in July 1998, **Instituto Ethos** (the Ethos Institute of Business and Social Responsibility) exists to promote the concept of socially responsible business behavior. More than eighty companies, mostly native to Brazil with some multinationals, have joined the institute. More companies are being recruited as part of a two-year strategic plan. The organization was fortunate to attract early support from a group of prominent business leaders who signed on as directors of the organization and took out corporate memberships. Advent of the institute corresponds to a general social concern in Brazil that corporations be active in addressing the country's serious social problems.

Instituto Ethos aims to identify and publicize leading examples of socially responsible business and promote models of good corporate citizenship. Activities undertaken or in progress include conferences, media outreach, demonstration projects, awards, university outreach, capacity-building technical assistance, and the promotion of trisector partnerships and exchanges. Outreach includes a direct mail survey of the business sector. Some one hundred and eighty participants attended the institute's first seminar. A select group of opinionmakers receive weekly information on corporate citizenship actions and issues.

Canada

In Canada, over four hundred and fifty companies are members of the **Imagine** program and are committed to giving at least 1 percent of net profits before taxes to community investment and to encourage employee involvement in social and community causes. Imagine also has 1,300 community partners and is the main forum for dialogue between the charitable and corporate sectors. An initiative of the **Canadian Centre for Philanthropy**, Imagine has a council of business advisers and is currently engaged in developing a new business-led agenda for corporate citizenship in Canada. This includes building a new framework for cross-sectoral partnerships and involving business more deeply in community building. Imagine advocates for corporate citizenship, serves to identify new models of partnership and collaboration, holds regular forums bringing together the business and the voluntary sectors, and provides access to resources for both businesses and charities seeking to form partnerships.

Chile

In Chile a published report by the **Chilean Benchmarking Group** has created momentum, particularly among young business leaders. Individual business leaders have sought to educate business people about social responsibility and business ethics, and there has been some support of CSOs at the community level. Although the political establishment has withheld its full support, a formal organization along the lines of the U.S.-based Business for Social Responsibility is expected to emerge soon.

India

In India, **Partners in Change** was created in 1995 to foster sustainable partnerships between the corporate sector and CSOs working to reduce poverty. Like the Thai organization TBIRD (described below), Partners in Change arose as an initiative of the civil society/CBO sector but works in conjunction with major Indian industry groups, corporate foundations, and national and grassroots CBOs. The program provides the institutional framework for the **Corporate Partnership** initiative of ActionAid, an international CSO.

Many Indian businesses have a strong tradition of contributing to society. The purpose of Corporate Partnership is to make it easy for companies—indigenous and multinational firms—to become involved in India's social development. To that end, Partners in Change advocates corporate involvement in social development, helps companies design citizenship and social responsibility actions, identifies reliable and effective CSO partners, monitors and evaluates projects, and offers management and training services. The program aims to document the work of socially responsible Indian companies and conducts surveys on corporate involvement. Among other activities, it publishes a magazine aimed at business and the mass media and a newsletter on disabilities. More than thirty companies have undertaken initiatives through the program.

Japan

Business is increasingly getting behind the civil society sector in Japan. Following the Hanshin-Awaji earthquake in 1995, in which civil society groups played a major relief role, the government worked with CSOs to introduce legislation to facilitate their incorporation and reduce state control over their activities. Debate over these legislative measures assembled an impressive coalition of government, business, and CSO leaders. This has led **Keidanren**, the Japan Federation of Economic Organizations comprising more than a thousand of the country's largest businesses, and influential CSOs to create the Japan NPO Center dedicated to promoting CSOs through cross-sectoral partnerships.

The Keidanren's Charter for Good Corporate Behavior, revised in 1996, specifically obligates members to behave in a socially responsible manner, in addition to respecting the letter and spirit of the law in countries where they operate. This injunction includes a commitment to "actively undertake philanthropic activities."

The Keidanren backed the establishment of the Council for Better Corporate Citizenship in 1989, which is mainly oriented toward encouraging Japanese firms to contribute to their host communities abroad, particularly in the United States, to ensure a smooth reception for Japanese firms in foreign countries. For example, the council has distributed a quarterly newsletter, *Stakeholders*, about the community relations activities of Japanese-affiliated firms in the United States. The Keidanren has conducted numerous study missions to explore other countries' approaches to corporate citizenship.

Mexico

In Mexico, more than two hundred institutions have become members of **MIRA**, the national program aimed at promoting corporate philanthropy and social investment. The **Centro Mexicano para la Filantropia (Mexican Center for Philanthropy)** started MIRA to further the Center's goal of encouraging social responsibility in the corporate sector and in society at large, and to strengthen civil institutions. To that end, the Center undertakes a range of campaigning, research, and institutional development programs. Operationally, the MIRA program works through four networks: CSOs, business, the media, and opinion leaders.

Namibia

In Namibia, the **Rossing Foundation** acts as an intermediary organization for channeling funds from international donor agencies, government, and businesses to CSOs and community-based organizations. Started by one company, it has evolved into something like an independent nationwide development agency funded by a range of sources. It offers twenty-five thousand Namibians the opportunity to complete classes in adult education, rural and community development, and maritime training from nine educational and agricultural centers around the country.

New Zealand

A new national initiative, **New Zealand Businesses for Social Responsibility**, has been incorporated in Auckland. This membership, nonprofit organization will disseminate information, hold conferences and seminars, and offer capacity development services to member firms.

Panama

Empresa Privada para Responsabilidad Social (BSR Panama) was launched in late 1998 and is in the process of identifying rising leaders in the Panamanian business community.

Philippines

Philippine Business for Social Progress (PBSP) is often cited as one of the best examples in the world of a business-led partnership that is tackling the problems of poverty and social unrest. It operates both at a grassroots level (by funding projects, capacity building, and sometimes directly running community projects) and at the strategic policy level (by influencing both corporate strategies and government policies).

A business-based organization, which is strongly influenced by civil society values, PBSP was founded in 1970 by a group of fifty firms that were alarmed by national economic decline, runaway inflation, growing poverty, social unrest, and political insurgency. Today it has a membership of nearly two hundred companies, undertakes projects for major international donors, conducts regular policy discussions with the Philippines government, and celebrates a proud history of having supported over three thousand projects throughout the country, involving some one thousand partner organizations and funding in the region of U.S.$50 million.

Although the organization has fundamentally restructured both its funding and operational strategies in light of experience and changed conditions, two founding principles have remained key to the organization's success and sustainability over nearly three decades:

- The melding of strong business discipline and equally strong social development expertise, and
- The active involvement of business supporters beyond the writing of checks (as important as these were, and to a lesser extent still are, to the organization's survival).

When it joins PBSP, each member company agrees in writing to follow several principles of corporate responsibility and specifically to set aside 1 percent of net income before taxes. Of this, 60 percent was originally channeled through PBSP and 40 percent was retained by the company for its own community investment activities. In 1989 this balance was changed to reflect the increasing desire of companies to manage their own community investment programs, with the result that today 20 percent is channeled through PBSP and 80 percent is retained by each member company (although in a number of cases, the companies then contract PBSP to run specific programs on their behalf). This funding structure allows for a clear delineation between funding operating costs and program costs, and gives member companies flexibility in how they balance their community spending as between their own corporate-managed projects and using PBSP as an intermediary organization.

Currently, the operations strategy is based on developing an integrated, multidisciplinary and resource-based approach to the challenge of poverty alleviation. The organization is also getting more involved in the policy debate and is taking a more strategic view and action perspective on the role of business in society, beyond philanthropy and community investment. To that end, PBSP engages in systematic, regular policy debate with the government on issues such as education, environment, and rural development.

In 1992 PBSP established the **Center for Corporate Citizenship in the Philippines**, which is specifically dedicated to promoting the practice and critical review of corporate citizenship among chief executive officers and other senior-level managers and decisionmakers in the country. For example, the Center supports research and holds an annual conference attended by the president of the Philippines or cabinet ministers and prominent leaders of the private sector. It also works with a number of chief executives through a series of consensus groups, which look at specific societal issues to which business can offer solutions in partnership with the public sector. Those issues have covered business and education, business and the environment, business and rural development, and business and local government. The Center is looking at core business policies and practices and their effect on society, the environment, and development in general.

Poland

The **Business Leaders Forum in Poland (BLFP)** was established in 1993 with support from The Prince of Wales Business Leaders Forum in the U.K. Its aim is to mobilize foreign and Polish companies to address issues critical to Poland's success as an emerging market economy and democratic society.

The BLFP works with its member companies and other partner organizations to demonstrate that environmental and social responsibility are, and should be, integral to core business activity. It helps publicize the wider social benefits of business, spread corporate good practice, and it helps build and publicize successful partnerships between the private sector and other groups in society. It strives to meet these objectives by designing and managing programs that companies can support both financially and in-kind; profiling and publicizing corporate good practice; and running regular meetings and consultations between companies, public officials, international visitors, and civil society organizations to discuss specific policy issues of project ideas.

Apart from a recently launched initiative on public safety in Warsaw, the BLFP has concentrated its programs on education, training, and youth initiatives, often working in partnership with other organizations. For example, "Autokreacja" is a youth leadership and development course based on a similar program run by the Prince's Trust in the United Kingdom.

The BLFP has also collected a wide range of case studies on corporate responsibility in Poland. These range from Coca-Cola's professional training support for the retail sector and its "whole village" recycling scheme, to projects such as American Express's customer service workshops and training program. Other case studies include ASS's state-of-the-art training center and its small-scale business development initiatives, which have helped over a hundred and twenty employees establish some fifteen new businesses as part of the ASS restructuring program; Huta Sendzimira's work in restructuring and managing change; BOC's welding school; and Commercial Union's banking and insurance training.

Thailand

The **Thai Business Initiative in Rural Development (TBIRD)** was launched in 1988 by the Population and Community Development Association of Thailand (PDA), one of the nation's leading CSOs. Through TBIRD, business firms in Thailand directly support community-based social and economic development in some of the poorest villages in Thailand's north and northeast. About a hundred companies—ranging from mid-sized Thai businesses to major multinationals with investments in Thailand—have been actively involved with TBIRD.

Like PBSP, TBIRD is often cited as a model for successful corporate engagement in a developing country. Both the Philippine and Thai initiatives contribute to the empowerment of community-based organizations and CSOs. Both provide frameworks for business involvement and facilitate partnership building.

TBIRD is essentially a network of partnerships between individual companies and individual villages. These partnerships are catalyzed, facilitated, supported, monitored and evaluated by PDA. With over twenty years of experience in rural grassroots development, PDA has pioneered some of the most effective integrated community-based development projects in Thailand, which are based on the principle that local participation and initiative are essential for self-reliant growth. Today, PDA operates a range of programs in water resource development, vocational training, HIV/AIDS prevention, education, income-generation, environmental conservation, population issues, and primary health care from its head office in Bangkok and its twelve rural development centers in northeastern and northern Thailand. It is therefore an ideal intermediary organization to promote the concept of corporate-community partnership to companies. The program helps to bring suitable partners together, facilitates corporate-community consultation and project planning, provides technical assistance, and coordinates with local government agencies and other CSO partners.

Project activities under TBIRD differ widely, depending on the needs, wishes, skills, and conditions of individual villages and companies. However, most activities encompass learning and skill development in four areas: organizational and financial management, production, and marketing. Agriculture-based income-generating activities are a key element in most projects. Alternatively, projects focus on income generation from cottage industries or small-scale business enterprises. The latter, in some cases, supply goods or services to the supporting company. Many projects also have a community development dimension. This can range from the establishment of small loan funds, to education support, vocational and computer training, environmental projects, and local infrastructure development.

United Kingdom

Arguably, the most comprehensive and largest of the national initiatives is **Business in the Community (BITC)** in Britain. When inner-city riots ripped through some of Britain's major urban areas in the early 1980s, the British business sector responded by becoming more proactive in tackling problems of rising unemployment, inequality, crime, and inner-city violence. The result was the establishment of Business in the Community in 1982.

BITC's mission is "to support the United Kingdom's economic and social regeneration by raising the quality and extent of business involvement in the community and making that involvement a natural part of successful business practice." To that end, BITC works through four hundred member companies and is governed by a board of thirty business, public, and voluntary sector leaders, including heads of the Confederation of British Industry, the Trades Union Congress, the National Council for Voluntary Organizations, and the Association of Metropolitan Authorities. BITC has about two hundred staff members based in London and in ten regional offices.

BITC currently runs nationwide campaigns on six themes: economic development, education, environment, employee involvement, Opportunity 2000 (aimed at employing more women and raising their status), and Race for Opportunity (aimed at boosting the economic activity of the U.K.'s ethnic minority communities). For each major initiative there is a leadership team, consisting of prominent business and community leaders as well as civil servants from relevant government departments, who champion and help to direct the program. This approach has been described as a critical factor in the success of the organization and of its campaigns.

In addition to facilitating business involvement in the community, Business in the Community has created programs to engage business attention and support. These include:

- Providers of professional services getting together in a Professional Firms Group to discuss ways in which these services can be offered for maximum impact to meet local community needs;
- The Per Cent Club, in which the companies that join pledge to contribute 0.5 percent of their domestic pretax profits or dividends to community investment;
- Awards programs that raise the profile of outstanding companies and the projects they are supporting;
- Advisory services on specific issues or to develop tailored programs;
- A business strategy group that advises on public policy and tracks economic and social trends relevant to companies and their community involvement;
- Seeing is Believing, a program for taking senior business executives on visits to corporate-community projects to inspire them into action.

The president of BITC is HRH The Prince of Wales.

Other Noteworthy Intermediate Initiatives

- Abrinq Foundation for the Rights of the Child, Brazil. Established in 1990 at the time of the World Summit for Children, this organization gathers fifteen hundred Brazilian companies involved in projects in favor of children's rights. It is supported by the contributions of more than a hundred members of the Brazilian Association of Toy Manufacturers.
- American Leadership Forum (ALF), Silicon Valley, United States. ALF is a nonprofit organization that enables senior-level leaders to work together to build philanthropy, public service, and community in Silicon Valley. The organization's Project Involve! has the mandate to increase the level of corporate community investment in Silicon Valley. The organization has produced several guides for developing strategies and finding resources for community programs. Through its one-year Fellows program, ALF is creating a strong regional network of key leaders across the private, public, and nonprofit sectors. Each year's class of twenty fellows is drawn equally from the private and voluntary sectors.
- Chihuahua Business Social Fund, Mexico. Thirty-five business organizations petitioned the state governor to increase business taxes by an additional 10 percent, resulting in 10 to 15 million pesos annually in new money, to be invested for charitable purposes by the Chihuahua Business Social Fund. The proposal became a decree in April 1994. Priorities were the establishment of nursing homes, orphanages, social assistance centers, and facilities for the disabled, with resources divided equally between programs in cities, in rural areas, and in native Indian communities.
- Friends of the Environment, Indonesia. Business leaders and environmental activists created this grantmaking organization to support environmental conservation and sustainable development.

Intermediate Initiatives with a Primary Emphasis on Assisting Private Sector Development

The "intermediate" initiatives described above are broad in scope and designed to engage the corporate sector in a wide range of social issues and concerns. Another feature of the landscape in a number of developing countries consists of intermediate initiatives established primarily to promote the development of the private sector, especially the growth and nurturing of small and medium indigenous enterprises (SMEs). Some examples of this trend are described in this section.

Egypt—The **Alexandria Business Association** in Egypt has operated a program to assist microentrepreneurs since 1983, using seed money supplied by the U.S. bilateral aid program. Similar initiatives of this kind, involving aid monies from various countries, can be found in other countries. Corporate-backed programs to support the development of minority group businesses are also found in some economically advanced countries such as the U.K., the United States, and Canada. They provide a vehicle for corporate engagement on a limited scale.

South Africa—The **Get Ahead Foundation** is one of several SME-focused intermediary initiatives supported by the business sector in South Africa. Established by Archbishop Desmond Tutu and others in 1984, it offers group-guaranteed microloans, technical assistance, skill development, and basic management training to thousands of informal sector entrepreneurs. In addition to being funded by the private sector, the foundation works with major companies like South African Breweries, Rio Tinto's Reef Training Centre and Middleburg Steel and Alloys to establish direct business and training linkages between large and small-scale enterprises.

Zimbabwe—**Partners for Growth** (**PfG**) in Zimbabwe exemplifies an effective business-led model of this kind. It provides a network and a focus for companies to contribute to the development of small firms by rendering advice, subcontracting, providing technical expertise and marketing support, and sponsoring enterprise education. The initiative also aids capacity development of Zimbabwean CSOs. Established in 1995 by business leaders with support from PWBLF and German and U.K. aid funds, this initiative by more than forty Zimbabwe business leaders aims to encourage the establishment of direct business linkages between large-scale companies and small indigenous enterprises. A number of program elements are involved, such as: helping to set up new small businesses and reinvigorating existing ones; helping to build the capacity of development agencies and CSOs; sharing experiences and communicating examples of successful partnerships within Zimbabwe and internationally; and improving the quality and opportunities for entrepreneurship. PfG produces a biannual publication of "good practice" case studies from Zimbabwe and around the world, and member companies come together regularly in small development teams to share experiences, to coordinate their involvement with other organizations, and to listen to international speakers.

Working in partnership with one of the country's leading government schools, PfG has recently launched an Enterprise Education program in nine schools as a pilot project. The program is modeled on similar initiatives in the U.K. and United States and the long-term goal is to expand its implementation throughout the country's school system.

National Business Associations as Intermediaries

A recent trend worth watching is the emergence of **corporate citizenship roles** in the mandates of some **national business associations.** In addition to traditional member service and trade association roles, some associations are becoming advocates for and facilitators of corporate citizenship.

An initiative by the **Confederation of Indian Industry (CII)** is indicative of this new trend. Representing more than three thousand Indian companies, CII has established a Corporate Citizenship Council concerned with education and literacy, health and family welfare, rural development, consumer affairs, sports, youth development, and HIV/AIDS prevention and cure. The HIV/AIDS program is a major communications and education and training initiative aimed at making the "business case" for corporate involvement in HIV/AIDS prevention and care and providing companies with the information and tools they need to take action. (HIV/AIDS is reported to be spreading faster in India than in any other country, and WHO estimates that, at current trends, by 2050 there will be more HIV positive people in India than in the rest of the world combined. This obviously has serious implications for Indian business.)

The association NCW is an independent affiliate of the Confederation of Netherlands Industry and Employers VNOI-NCW, the largest employers' federation of the Netherlands, which represents eighty thousand Dutch companies. Through an active seminar and conference program, the **Management Center for Corporate Community Involvement of NCW** brings together industry, labor, government, and the social sector. Subjects covered range from community investment to human rights and labor conditions in supplier countries.

MULTILATERAL PROGRAMS THAT PROMOTE CORPORATE CITIZENSHIP AND ENGAGEMENT

Multilateral lending agencies like the World Bank, regional development banks and UNDP have become interested in corporate citizenship in recent years.

The World Bank Group

The World Bank is seeking to involve business in addressing a range of social, environmental, and economic concerns. The Bank's Finance and Private Sector Division declared September 12, 1996, Corporate Citizenship

Day and organized a seminar preceding the annual IMF/World Bank annual meetings. Over five hundred people attended the seminar, which brought together senior decisionmakers from business, CSOs, and foundations with their counterparts in the World Bank Group (WBG) to review good practices and discuss future private-public partnerships for social development. A major World Bank-supported program has resulted from the discussions surrounding this event.

Business Partners for Development

Business Partners for Development (BPD) is an informal global network of businesses, civil society organizations, and relevant government ministries, with the World Bank Group as an equal partner. BPD aims to produce solid evidence of the positive impact of trisector partnerships—both the developmental impact and the business impact. BPD intends to demonstrate that these partnerships for development:

- provide win-win benefits to all three parties;
- can be much more widely used throughout the world;
- can be scaled up to national and regional levels.

On June 9, 1998, the Board of the World Bank Group formally approved participation in the BPD proposal, and U.S.$3 million in support over the three-year period. This grant will represent no more than 15 percent of the total budget. Over sixty companies, civil society organizations, and others have agreed to participate in the initiative to date.

BPD is structured around four sectoral clusters: natural resource industries, water, youth, and road traffic safety. Each cluster is convened by leaders from the three partners—business, civil society and state—with support from the World Bank Group. The representatives from each cluster select three to four focus projects. Participants apply the practical and policy lessons learned from this collaboration in their ongoing partnership work. Each of the four clusters is freestanding, though linked to the broader BPD network. A fifth cluster, the Knowledge Resource Group, was established to ensure that learning from each cluster feeds across into the other clusters and into the larger learning and sharing campaign on trisector partnerships.

- The **Natural Resources Cluster** held three meetings in Washington, D.C., in 1998 co-convened by BP (now BP-Amoco), CARE International, and the WBG, and chaired by BP. CARE is hosting the secretariat. Twelve companies from the oil and mining industries attended the cluster meetings along with three representatives from civil society. Focus projects were agreed in

Colombia, Indonesia, and Venezuela. Others were proposed in the Caspian Sea region, India, Papua New Guinea, the Philippines, South Africa, and Zimbabwe. In all cases, potential implications will be discussed with the relevant WBG country team before final decisions are made.

- On June 4, 1998, the first meeting of the **Youth and Education Cluster** (the Global Partnership for Youth Development) was held in Washington, D.C. The meeting was co-convened by the Kellogg Company, the International Youth Foundation, and the WBG. Four companies participated (and thirteen others expressed their commitment to take part in subsequent meetings) along with six representatives from civil society and bilateral aid agencies. The participants discussed a vision for the work and the objective of the cluster, with a proposed millennium linkage. In addition to focus projects, ideas for global youth initiatives were discussed, such as organizing a global children's day and the idea to contribute the "last hours' wage" as a fundraising campaign toward youth development. Further cluster meetings took place in Chicago, hosted by Lions Clubs International and Iridium LLC. Major corporate backers of the Youth and Education Cluster are Kellogg's, Lions Clubs International, Nike, Shell and Petroleos de Venezuela, American Express, Cisco Systems, the International Youth Foundation, Financial Times, Hill & Knowlton, and Microsoft.
- The **Water and Sanitation Cluster** held meetings in March, June, September, and December 1998 in Paris and London and by videoconference. The meetings were co-convened by Générale des Eaux (Vivendi), WaterAid, and the WBG. Eight companies participated along with nine representatives from civil society. Focus projects were agreed in Argentina, Bolivia, Colombia, Haiti, Indonesia, and South Africa. In all cases, operational costs are born by the sponsoring corporation, totaling an estimated U.S.$3 million per year. WaterAid in the U.K. is hosting the secretariat.
- A **Road Safety Cluster** (Global Road Safety Partnership) was conceived in late 1998 and development meetings began early in 1999. The International Red Cross is hosting the secretariat, and many government agencies, CSOs, and companies are working to develop this cluster and its programming. This cluster will test the trisector partnership approach to assist in reducing mortality rates from road traffic accidents—projected to be the world's third leading cause of death by 2020. The first meeting was held in October 1998.

- On June 26, 1998, a planning group met in Washington, D.C., to consider options for a cross-cutting **Knowledge Resource Group** (KRG). Eighteen organizations attended this meeting. The KRG is co-convened by CIVICUS, The Prince of Wales Business Leaders Forum, and the WBG. CIVICUS hosts the secretariat and administers the funds for this cluster. Participants have focused on clarifying their role in assisting the process of connecting and collecting knowledge of trisector partnerships, so that practitioners become aware of, and try to improve on, what is being done elsewhere. The KRG's activities include:
  - Program development: identifying professional services that clusters may draw upon to help meet technical partnership needs of the focus project;
  - Quick response and troubleshooting: identifying direct assistance to unexpected difficulties that may otherwise put a partnership at risk;
  - Action learning: offering help in systematically developing joint study visits;
  - Action research: offering research assistance on identified partnership challenges, part-funding independent research on generic partnership challenges, and helping extract generalized lessons from each cluster's work;
  - Communications: aggregating and disseminating knowledge, in conjunction with others.

As the BPD network evolves, a number of options for possible KRG and cluster participation include:

- Focus projects.
- National roundtables/workshops in each country with a focus project: The objective will be to present the focus project and to analyze it within the context of the government's development strategy as well as within the context of other partnerships for development within that country. Businesses may wish to participate in those national roundtables where they have operations or interests in that country.
- Practitioner study visits. These visits provide an opportunity for partnership project practitioners to work laterally with their global peer group in the focus projects. This practical forum will offer cross-fertilization of ideas and exchange of experiences, with

follow-up commitments. Each study visit will have a limited number of places reserved for additional practitioners.

- Training/capacity building. A range of options has been proposed for focus projects: for example, partnership formation; participatory project management; conflict prevention and resolution; options for local partnership agreements; and operating procedures for local government for working in partnership with community organizations and the private sector. In many cases training will be integrated with a study visit program.
- Knowledge management. Research relevant to the network, perhaps in collaboration with other participating organizations.
- Dissemination of Outputs. Learning outputs will be available from the four clusters, and from the Knowledge Resource Group. A website for the BPD network has been created. It will contain details about all outputs, tools that have been tried, terms of reference and specifications that have been used successfully, and a database of projects, alongside links to related websites of all network participants.

It is important to note that most of the focus projects would happen with or without BPD. However, participation with BPD is expected to enhance the positive impact of these projects for the participating companies and communities. The case for the added value of BPD cuts across the clusters in several important ways (as identified by corporate members of BPD):

- BPD provides a forum in which to address a variety of contentious issues;
- BPD is a mutually leveraged instrument that provides the opportunity for momentum that would not otherwise exist;
- BPD provides an umbrella, convening groups that would not otherwise be partners;
- BPD allows participants to share the risks, rather than carry the risk of operating alone;
- The World Bank Group's role in BPD will help companies transcend issues of competition and work more easily with host governments; and
- BPD will help spread the learning and enable more efficient ways of working through partnership.

If BPD operates as envisioned, it will assist each member of the BPD network and will increase the positive developmental impact.

Business Partners for Development Clusters

- Natural Resources
- Water and Sanitation
- Global Partnership for Youth Development
- Global Road Safety Partnership
- Knowledge Resource Group

United Nations Development Program

The Private Sector Development Program (PSDP) at UNDP supports the efforts of UNDP in the area of employment and sustainable livelihoods by providing expertise in enterprise development and microfinance. This office also supports UNDP Country Office efforts in broader private sector development. As part of its overall strategy, PSDP works as a catalyst to engage the private sector for substantial collaboration and resource mobilization to build public and private partnerships.

The Global Sustainable Development Facility

The objective of the **Global Sustainable Development Facility (GSDF)** is to develop and design a framework for cooperation between the UNDP and the corporate sector, based on the **2B2M/2020** vision (bringing two billion people to the global market economy by the year 2020). This new framework, or facility, aims to support innovative and practical actions that will meet UNDP's goals of sustainable human development, poverty alleviation, and a civic society, while providing necessary incentives for the private sector.

The immediate objectives of the project are:

- To convene a dialogue between corporations and UNDP that will increase the understanding and knowledge of each other,
- To examine examples of cooperation between corporations and public organizations to identify successful and mutually beneficial approaches for cooperation, and
- To undertake activities that will test and illustrate the potential for cooperative action between business and the international public sector represented by UNDP.

At the completion of the project, a new cooperation framework, or facility, will be launched. The objectives, activities, and constitution of this facility are being jointly formulated through a process involving consultative workshops (three have been held since October 1998: in New York, Miami, and Cape Town), demonstration projects, interviews with corporations, and the practical definition and design of the new facility.

A Corporate Advisory Council is providing inputs to the GSDF Steering Committee on critical issues relating to the project. The Council membership includes representatives of ABB Group, AT&T, Cultor Corporation, Dow Chemical, ESKOM, Hennes & Mauritz, IKEA International, LM Ericsson, Novartis, Owens Corning, Oracle, Rio Tinto, RWE, Statoil, Swedbank, and Telia AB.

A UNDP project team is managing the implementation of the GSDF project. The rationale for a strategic engagement between the business community and the development community is that, in the long term, a strong relationship exists between sustainable development and the growth of shareholder value.

Money Matters Institute

UNDP's Money Matters Institute is a working committee of senior executives from private financial firms and public officials from the UN system and developing countries. The Money Matters Institute focuses on best practices in two research areas: how can private capital be used for sustainable human development, and what is needed in developing countries to attract and retain such private capital and transform it into development?

International Labor Organization (Geneva)

The Social Transformation and Enterprise Performance in a Global Economy Project

The **World Business Academy**, in collaboration with the **International Labor Organization** and the **International Institute of Labor Studies**, has launched an initiative called **STEP** (the Social Transformation and Enterprise Performance in a Global Economy Project). According to its sponsors, STEP aims to provide managers with down-to-earth knowledge and practical tools for improving the performance of business in a socially responsible business manner.

The STEP project will begin with a comprehensive global research study into best practices that mutually support social responsibility, performance improvement, and the development of human capital. Training programs will be offered in a number of developing and formerly Communist countries. STEP also aims to identify and promote opportunities for firms to link with other social partners, such as employer groups, trade unions, CSOs, business schools, government institutions, and international agencies in strategic alliances. The aim is to improve the ways in which business performance can benefit the wider community. Its sponsors claim that this project offers great potential for both dialogue and action.

CORPORATE PARTICIPATION IN POLICY DIALOGUE ON SOCIAL AND OTHER ISSUES THAT AFFECT CIVIL SOCIETY

A trend of growing importance is the increasing involvement of the business sector in the policy debates surrounding social, economic, and environmental policies. The business sector is engaging in policy dialogue in an increasingly systematic manner.

Over the last few years, many new business coalitions and public-private task forces have been established at local, national, and international levels to address such issues as policies for microenterprise development, education, youth development, environment, health, and related welfare issues. The following are a few examples of business engagement in policy dialogue.

International Level

The **Caux Round Table.** This informal grouping of over one hundred senior business leaders from North America, Europe, and Japan believes that the world business community should play an important role in improving economic and social conditions. It has met once or twice a year since 1986 and has issued "an international ethics code for business" and other declarations. It aims to promote extensive corporate support for social responsibility and business identification with global concerns of interest to civil society, such as sustainable development.

The **International Chamber of Commerce** (**ICC**). This organization represents the voice of business in many international gatherings. The ICC is now active in areas such as sustainable development and anti-corruption policies. The ICC's principles for environmental management were codified as the Business Charter for Sustainable Development, adopted by the ICC Executive Board in November 1990.

The **World Business Council for Sustainable Development** (**WBCSD**) has already been referred to in an earlier section. It is actively engaged in policy discussions regarding climate change and water and is an interlocutor with international bodies on these subjects.

National Level

At the national level, public-private dialogue is occurring around a wide variety of nontraditional issues. Many of these initiatives are thematic.

- Many public-private national councils for sustainable development have been established since the 1992 Rio Earth Summit.
- National business councils are engaging in policy dialogue on HIV/AIDS in Thailand, Zimbabwe, and India.
- Welfare-to-work government and business task forces have been established in the U.K. and the United States.
- The China Employee Benefits Forum looks at employment policies.

More General Change-Oriented National Initiatives Involving Business

Other public-private consultation structures are more general and address a range of integrated development and societal issues. The following are examples of such initiatives.

In Ghana the **Private Enterprise Foundation** is implementing a nationwide capacity-building program (the National Capacity Development and Utilization Program) cooperatively with the government, UNDP, ILO, and five national agencies representing business and civil society. The focus has been on public-private policy dialogue and the leveraging of both public and private resources to generate employment and enhanced income opportunities.

In 1995 a group of Peruvian business leaders, representing national and foreign companies, and supported by the Confederation Nacional de Instituciones Empresariales Privadas (CONFIEP), established the **Peru 2021** initiative. This aims to promote a new national vision of business leadership working in partnership with the government. A secondary goal is to foster the development of policies and projects needed to create a modern, internationally competitive economy and a decent quality of life for all Peruvians by the bicentennial year 2021. The initiative has identified a set of key themes for which it is developing vision statements for the year 2021, consultations and focus groups, surveys, and joint public-private action plans. These themes include leadership, education, the economy, the environment, technology, society, government, and business. Initiatives are under way relating to education, sustainable development, and social responsibility. Activities have included a conference and seminar in Lima on corporate social responsibility in March and December 1998 respectively. Currently in preparation is a book on the same subject and a corporate leadership award.

The **National Business Initiative for Growth, Development, and Democracy in South Africa** is supported by 175 leading private companies. It aims to produce practical frameworks, innovative policy ideas, and institutional innovations to help both local and national government in different aspects of public administration and policymaking. Among the programs managed by NBI is **Business Against Crime (BAC)**, launched by Business South Africa, the umbrella organization for all the country's chambers of commerce. This program is based on the belief that while many individual companies are applying substantial resources to combat and prevent crime and corruption, the collective application or coordination of these efforts will be more effective and efficient than individual action. BAC is helping the government design an integrated criminal justice information management system; it is aiding companies to combat commercial crime; it is working with car maker BMW to improve the quality of highway patrol vehicles and equipment; and it is designing new management and training systems for police stations. In all cases, private sector firms are working to address these issues with the public sector.

The **Shanghai Business Leadership 2000 Program** was established in 1996 as a partnership between the mayor of Shanghai, Shanghai Jiao Tong University, and a group of major international companies operating in China, including Coopers & Lybrand, BOC Gases, ERM, McKinsey, Coca-Cola, Sedgwick, DHL, John Swire & Sons, Marks & Spencer, and G. Melchers & Co. Initially conceived as a short-term, part-time program for senior managers from international companies and their counterparts in Chinese state-owned enterprises, the program is now being evaluated. Eight weekly sessions focused on problem-solving and management skills such as cross-cultural business challenges in key business disciplines, new approaches to human resource development, leveraging information technology, global marketing, total quality management, corporate governance, and business environmental management issues. Case studies relevant to China were discussed and the managers participated in joint project visits. The program's mission is to promote cross-cultural understanding among Chinese and Western business leaders and to help manage dramatic economic and social change. At the program's core is a two-way process of mutual learning that acknowledges the value of the business practices that Western managers can share with their Chinese counterparts, while recognizing the strengths of Chinese culture and society. It is hoped that the alumni group can work effectively together to promote good corporate citizenship in Shanghai.

Municipal or Urban Level

At the local level, business is getting involved in policy dialogue and joint action with local authorities in unprecedented ways. In some cities, the need for urban renewal is a strong motivating force, in others the issue is how to manage massive growth. Many cities have adopted "Local Agenda 21" processes (encouraged by the 1992 Rio Earth Summit), which call for conscious efforts to address local sustainable development issues collaboratively.

Examples of major urban partnership initiatives involving both policy participation and action include:

- Cleveland 2000 (USA),
- Krakow Development Forum (Poland),
- Hong Kong Private Sector Committee of the Environment (Hong Kong), and
- Central Johannesburg Partnership (South Africa).

Sectoral Initiatives

There are also a number of policy-oriented sectoral initiatives. For example:

- The World Travel and Tourism Council has established a major policy program looking at sustainable tourism.
- The global insurance industry is involved in policy analysis on biodiversity issues.
- A global coalition has been formed to discuss financial policy issues related to the environment. The coalition comprises private global financial institutions, along with some smaller banks from emerging markets and the multilateral development banks.

The UN Environment Program has played a role in setting up both the insurance and financial initiatives. Some two hundred organizations are involved in these two programs.

MEMBERSHIP-BASED, CAPACITY-BUILDING ORGANIZATIONS WITH A FOCUS ON DEVELOPING CORPORATE SOCIAL RESPONSIBILITY AND CITIZENSHIP

A number of membership-based business organizations in Europe, the United States, and Canada offer services to their members in the area of corporate citizenship and social responsibility. These organizations help companies develop, manage, evaluate, and realize value from their corporate citizenship activities and provide networking opportunities with like-minded firms. They also produce useful resources for developing and implementing programs.

Business for Social Responsibility (USA)

Founded in 1992, **Business for Social Responsibility (BSR)** is a national association of businesses, with more than fourteen hundred members and affiliated members. Collectively, BSR members have annual revenues that total U.S.$1 trillion and they employ nearly five million workers. BSR provides assistance to companies seeking to implement policies and practices that contribute to the long-term, sustained, and responsible success of their enterprise and that fairly balance the competing claims of key stakeholders, their investors, employees, customers, business partners, communities, and the environment. Many of BSR's members are medium- and small-scale companies that are rarely represented on organizations of this type.

BSR operates as an alliance of companies, with a board of directors drawn from a combination of major companies and small-scale, entrepreneurial start-ups. It has offices in Washington D.C., San Francisco, Boston, and Denver and is funded by its membership fees and other voluntary contributions from corporations and corporate foundations.

- BSR operates the **Business for Social Responsibility Education Fund (BSREF)**, a nonprofit research, education, and advocacy organization to promote more responsible practices in the broader business community, beyond BSR's immediate membership.
- BSR's **Business and Human Rights Program** helps companies address the broad range of human rights issues they face in sourcing and manufacturing in developing countries—for example, worker health and safety, child labor, prison labor, wages and hours, working conditions, and environmental standards. Technical assistance and consulting is offered to help companies develop and implement corporate human rights policies. The program provides educational workshops and training sessions and facilitates dialogue between the business community, human rights organizations, government officials, and labor unions. It carries out research and publishes materials concerning global resourcing and human rights. And it is creating a print and online database of corporate "best practices" on these issues.

- Additionally, BSR operates programs on **Business and the Environment, Workplace Policies and Practices, Community Involvement, and Affirmative Action**. In May 1996, it played a role in helping to convene the White House Conference on Corporate Citizenship.

BSR's membership services include:

- Research—including "best practice" research on a range of issues such as employee benefits and global code of conduct;
- A regular newsletter, reports, and a recent book entitled *Beyond the Bottom Line*;
- Conferences, meetings, and seminars—including a national annual conference attended by some five hundred leaders from business, government, and the nonprofit sector;
- Issues monitoring and advocacy—through monitoring the media, and regular contact with public officials, advocacy groups, member companies, and others;
- Technical assistance and advice—including the sharing of tools and models for analyzing and improving corporate policies and practices, such as company social responsibility self-assessments and comprehensive environmental audits;
- Outreach and education—with other business organizations, elected and appointed public officials, advocacy and public interest groups, scholars, community leaders, and the media;
- Public Policy—BSR informs members about a limited number of key national public policy issues and produces a quarterly report covering these, although BSR itself does not take positions on public policy issues;
- Publicity for members' business products, services, and "best practices";
- Business-to-business exchange; and
- Establishment of regional networks.

BSR has inspired the creation of counterpart organizations in Canada, Panama, Chile, and other countries in Latin America. It financially supported the Conference on Business Social Responsibility in the Americas and assisted in the creation of EMPRESA, the regional forum on business and social responsibility.

Centre for Tomorrow's Company (U.K.)

The **Centre for Tomorrow's Company** is the outcome of a two-year business-led inquiry into the future of British business that looked at key factors for long-term competitive business success. The Tomorrow's Company inquiry was an initiative of the Royal Society of Arts and was chaired by Sir Anthony Cleaver, head of IBM U.K. The panel held hearings around Britain and attracted tremendous interest from the private sector. The enquiry report, published in 1995, called on U.K. business leaders to take an "inclusive" approach to managing relations with key stakeholders, including the community. The center was established after publication of the report. It assists its members to develop stakeholder management skills. An investment fund has also been set up to invest in companies that subscribe to the Tomorrow's Company management model.

The Conference Board (USA and Canada)

The **Conference Board organizations in the USA and Canada** have long provided research, networking, and professional development services in corporate community involvement for their members as well as tracking corporate performance.

Since April 1997 the U.S. Conference Board has administered the Ron Brown Award for Corporate Citizenship, awarded annually by the U.S. president. The Board's annual "Best in Class Award" has recognized corporate involvement in improving primary and secondary education since 1991. The Board holds regular seminars and workshops on developing corporate-giving policies and goals, designing contributions budgets, and benchmarking and evaluating corporate-giving programs. A conference entitled "Global Corporate Citizenship" took place early in 1999. Topics covered in recent reports include the measurement of the community involvement of companies, international programs of U.S. firms, and strategic opportunities in community activity. The Conference Board also maintains a database on the annual contributions budgets of U.S. corporations. The U.S. Board's Contributions Management Institute awards a certificate of achievement for attendance at three seminars or workshops.

In June 1998 the U.S. Conference Board, the Conference Board of Canada, and the United States Department of Education started work on a research project on the benefits to employers and employees of workplace education.

The **Canadian Centre for Business in the Community** (CCBC), a unit of the Conference Board of Canada, provides professional development services to members in the areas of corporate responsibility and ethics, corporate community investment, community economic development, and partnerships and alliances. CCBC is currently engaged in a "best practice" study of corporate social responsibility among more than a dozen large corporations operating in Canada.

Council on Foundations (USA)

Founded in 1949, the primary mission of the **Council on Foundations** is as a nonprofit membership association of grantmaking foundations, its primary mission being to promote responsible and effective philanthropy. The Council's Corporate Citizenship Project, with sixteen corporate participants, has focused on developing a comprehensive framework for measuring the impact of corporate citizenship on business performance. In 1996 it published a case study report on seven company programs that illustrate how businesses can add value to their corporate community involvement.

Social Venture Network (USA and Europe)

Founded in the United States in 1987, the **Social Venture Network (SVN)** has grown from a handful of visionary individuals to a vibrant grouping of more than four hundred and fifty business owners, investors, and social activists. This U.S.-based international organization of successful business and social entrepreneurs is dedicated to changing the way the world does business and to using its influence to promote progressive solutions to social problems. SVN offers conferences, events, and publications on business and sustainable development, public policy, social equity, and other issues. It works with businesses to place graduate students in related jobs and internships.

SVN takes credit for four direct offspring: Business for Social Responsibility, the Investors' Circle, Students for Responsible Business (see below), and a Latin American Network.

Social Venture Network Europe was launched in Amsterdam in 1993 with the support of the U.S. organization. It is involved in a range of social and environmental projects, thereby publicly advancing the case for ethical business practices. Activities include:

- Developing SVN Standards for Corporate Responsibility. This major international project, jointly organized with SVN U.S. and involving member companies and expert advisers, aims to develop standards and practical tools that help companies assess their ac-

tions in a wide range of areas such as ethics, governance, community involvement, employee development, and sustainable development.
- Supporting Human Rights Watch in the establishment of its Brussels office and in developing the European press office. This has helped the organization have a major influence on the European Union and its member states.
- Setting up the Trade Development Alliance to combine the expertise of CSOs in the area of fair trade with the business skills and contacts of companies, so that small groups of producers in poor countries can be linked to mainstream companies.
- PYMWYMIC (Put Your Money Where Your Mouth Is Company), a venture capital fund set up in 1994 to invest in companies whose policies and operations align with SVN Europe's aims and values.

SVN Europe is planning to launch:

- The SVN Europe Investors' Circle, to bring together SVN members, investors, and financial institutions to further responsible investing internationally.
- "YES" a support network for students and young professionals committed to corporate responsibility. This project, run in conjunction with AIESEC and the New Academy of Business, will offer work experience, mentoring and projects in members' companies.

Students for Responsible Business

Students for Responsible Business (SRB) emerged from the collaborative leadership of seventeen graduate business students who met during the summer of 1993, while participating in an internship program sponsored by the Social Venture Network. Through this program, students were matched with SVN member companies and given the opportunity to apply their business skills while learning about the stakeholder approach to business management. By the end of the summer, the interns decided to create a new organization of graduate business students who were committed to exploring the theory and practice of responsible business.

Within a few months, this core group of leaders held a founding conference at Georgetown University in Washington, D.C. The success of the conference went beyond the founders' expectations. The one hundred forty conference participants returned to their business schools to establish chapters of a new organization whose mission is to transform the way business is taught and practiced in the future.

SRB has grown significantly since then. There are currently more than thirteen hundred members representing one hundred graduate business schools throughout North America, of which eleven hundred are affiliated with one of forty-five established chapters. With another ten chapters in the start-up phase and growing interest from European, Asian, and South American business schools, SRB is maintaining its rapid growth curve. In the midst of this growth, however, the primary goals are to foster alignment throughout the network, collaboration among chapters, and engagement with the major issues and opportunities confronting today's business leaders.

RESEARCH AND TEACHING INSTITUTIONS SPECIALIZING IN CORPORATE CITIZENSHIP AND RELATED ISSUES

Academic institutions in several countries have established centers for teaching and research in the area of corporate citizenship.

The **Boston College Center for Corporate Community Relations** is part of the college's Wallace E. Caroll School of Management. The Center provides professional development to prepare all levels of management for expanding community relations responsibilities, custom training either at the college or at a business site, research and consulting on developing community relations policies, a Resource Center on Corporate Citizenship that houses materials from hundreds of corporations, a newsletter on community relations trends, an international leaders conference, and the Community Relations Online Forum. The Center's hallmark program is the "Neighbor of Choice" strategy for managing community relations.

The **Corporate Citizenship Unit** of the Centre for Corporate Strategy and Change at **Warwick Business School** in Britain was established in October 1996, with the initial support of BP, to develop research into and teaching of the role of business in society—specifically, how and why companies contribute to sustainable development by acting as socially responsible corporate citizens. Chris Marsden, its interim head, was formerly BP's community affairs manager. The Unit works closely with The Prince of Wales Business Leaders Forum, the New Economics Foundation, Business Partners for Development, and the Worldwide Fund for Nature. The Unit also sponsors an e-mail list with several hundred subscribers called "teaching-corporate-citizenship." It serves as a "virtual community" for academics and practitioners interested in pursuing research and teaching on citizenship and community involvement in business schools.

The **Institute for Social Responsibility** is an organized research unit of San Jose State University. It seeks to provide a source of information and training on issues of business ethics and social responsibility within the academic, business, and civic communities of Northern California. The Institute sponsors lecture series, conferences, working papers, and training sessions on topical issues in social responsibility. Matching resources to needs, the Institute strives to act as a liaison between the profit and nonprofit sectors of the Silicon Valley in California by giving pro bono services for nonprofit companies in need and helping locate avenues of action for commercial firms interested in social responsibility and community improvement.

The **New Business Academy** was founded in 1995 by The Body Shop International with the goal of developing the kind of business education required for socially and ecologically responsible business. It is researching best practice case studies and developing programs for current and future business executives in subjects like social and ethical auditing, ecomanagement, socially responsible business, international trade and human rights, and renewing corporate governance.

Other academic centers with an emerging interest in this field include **Deakin University** in Victoria, Australia; the **Norwegian School of Economics and Business** Administration at Bergen, Norway; and **Maastricht University** in the Netherlands.

SELECTED PRIVATE CONSULTANCIES SUPPORTING LEADERSHIP INITIATIVES IN CORPORATE ENGAGEMENT

Mention should also be made of certain private consultancies and networks that support the development of leadership initiatives.

London Benchmarking Group

The **London Benchmarking Group (LBG)** was formed in September 1994 by six companies with substantial community involvement programs: BP, Diageo, IBM, Marks & Spencer, Nat West Group, and Whitbread. The companies felt a need for accurate and comparable information about how different companies define, fund, and manage their community involvement activities. The Group's goal is defined in its mission statement as: "to better define the measures of efficiency and effectiveness of all types of community involvement activity by using benchmarking techniques."

Group members initially looked at their own work with a view to evolving a definitive benchmarking approach that would improve the quality and effectiveness of their programs. Additional companies have since joined in a wider measurement project under LBG's auspices. The Group's work has included, for example, the creation of a template and methodology for classifying and measuring the value of corporate community contributions, tools for evaluating the impact on society, and a suggested methodology for reporting on these contributions to company stakeholders.

The Corporate Citizenship Company

The **Corporate Citizenship Company**, based in London, England, aims to help corporations manage their global social responsibilities and community involvement activities to maximum effect, through advice on policy, management, evaluation, and benchmarks. The firm's work includes three reports on corporate citizenship practices involving employees and the drafting of the Code of Principles and Practice for the Global Council on HIV and AIDS. The company was founded as a result of a February 1997 partnership between the consulting firm Corporate Citizenship International, run by David Logan, and the community affairs consultant and publisher of *Community Affairs Briefing*, Michael Tuffrey. Mr. Logan is coauthor, with Delwin Roy and Laurie Regelbrugge, of the seminal 1997 report *Global Corporate Citizenship—Rationale and Strategies*, published by The Hitachi Foundation in Washington, D.C.

SustainAbility

SustainAbility is a U.K.-based think tank and consultancy that works with major companies around the world, helping them to realign their corporate strategy to the sustainable development agenda. It promotes the concept of the "Triple Bottom Line—economic, environmental, and social" and is playing an influential role in moving the corporate agenda in this direction.

Its "Engaging Stakeholders" program, begun in 1995, builds on earlier work carried out by SustainAbility and the UN Environment Program (UNEP) in the area of corporate environmental reporting. It was based on the active support of sixteen sponsoring companies, and more than twelve stakeholder organizations—ranging from stock exchanges to institutional investors and government—whose work increasingly involves using the environmental reports produced by companies worldwide. The program has a triple focus:

- the growing need for business to engage a range of internal and external stakeholders in developing and implementing sustainable development programs;
- the role of environmental disclosure and reporting in building the necessary credibility, trust, and other forms of 'social capital'

needed to ensure real, sustained stakeholder relationships that genuinely add value to a particular business; and, more specifically,

- the role of the corporate environmental report (CER) in addressing both these areas of need.

Professional Service Firms

The "ethical decisionmaking" service developed by **KMPG** is an example of how major global management consulting firms are developing services to train corporate executives to take moral factors into account in business decisions. KMPG suggests that executives need to be trained in ethical decisionmaking and has identified six major steps for this process. **PriceWaterhouseCoopers** is another global firm that is developing tools to aid firms in ethical decisionmaking and reputation management.

Other Firms and Foundations

A growing range of private firms provides specialized services to business in the field of corporate citizenship and responsibility. These firms include, in the U.K., **Bruce Naughton Wade**, which compiles a "corporate community involvement index," and in the United States, **Walker Information** and **SmithOBrien**, firms that are advancing the measurement and benchmarking of corporate involvement performance. Other groups like the **Institute for Development Research** (USA) and the **New Economics Foundation** (U.K.) are making intellectual contributions that are highly relevant to the emerging models of business-civil society collaboration.

SELECTED OTHER ORGANIZATIONS

Business Enterprise Trust (USA)

The **Business Enterprise Trust** is a national, nonprofit organization that promotes social leadership in business. Through the annual Business Enterprise Awards, the Trust honors business leaders who creatively combine sound management with social conscience.

Founded in 1989 by eighteen prominent leaders in American business, academia, labor, and the media, the Trust believes that a strong, competitive private enterprise system is the foundation of national economic prosperity and the cornerstone of personal and political liberty. In 1991 the Trust initiated the Business Enterprise Awards. Recipients are honored at an annual ceremony attended by business and academic leaders, and given wide exposure in the national media. The Trust also produces short video documentaries, monographs, and business school cases on the award recipients. These educational materials are said to be in use in hundreds of business schools, universities, and corporate training programs. The Trust also maintains a database of best practice case studies.

Council on Economic Priorities (USA)

Established in 1975, the **Council on Economic Priorities (CEP)** in the United States rates companies on issues like environmental stewardship and treatment of employees. The foundation of their research is to hold companies responsible—for their employees, their customers, and their own actions, so that consumers may take action through company boycotts to promote change and corporate responsibility. The CEP has posited that corporations with a track record of ethical decisionmaking will do better in the marketplace and win public respect by demonstrating good corporate citizenship.

CEP focuses its research on all the factors that make up the social framework of a company: the quality of management, its leadership among industry peers, its workplace climate. Their work encompasses the many aspects of ethical performance, including human rights, equal employment opportunity, concern for the environment, and strong involvement in the community. The corporation that continues to review the social health of its policies and takes a proactive stance on substantive issues is most likely already a Corporate Conscience Award winner or a CEP Honor Roll Company. Most such companies are strong across the board, reflecting social consciousness from the top down.

In early 1997 the **Council on Economic Priorities Accreditation Agency (CEPAA)** was established as a nonprofit affiliate of the CEP. *Business Week* magazine (October 20, 1997) acclaimed the new Agency as "a potential breakthrough not just on sweatshops, but on common labor standards for the global economy as a whole." CEPAA aims to drive the development of a universal standard to ensure that business practices for auditing and certification of labor practices evolve in a responsible manner, and to provide comparable data internationally. Representatives of unions, human rights and children's rights groups, academia, retailers, manufacturers, contractors, as well as consulting, accounting, and certification firms are helping to develop a draft standard, Social Accountability 8000 (SA 8000).

International Association for Business and Society

The **International Association for Business and Society (IABS)** is a learned society devoted to research and teaching on the relationships between business and society. Founded in 1990, it now comprises more than three hundred professors worldwide, from one hundred universities in twenty countries. IABS is a multidisciplinary association. It attracts scholars from all the disciplines of management. Its research domain covers the various aspects of the interface between management and the social and political dynamics of the surrounding society. It includes, among others, research on corporate social responsibility and performance, emerging social issues for business, business ethics, environmental affairs, and business and government relations. In partnership with Roosevelt University and Sage Publications, IABS publishes *Business & Society*, the only refereed journal devoted exclusively to business and society research. The Association also organizes an annual conference, which alternatively meets two years in North America and one year outside of North America. Papers presented at the conference are selected through a blind review process, and are published in the conference proceedings.

Maxwell Brem is director of communications for the Imagine Program of the Canadian Centre for Philanthropy. He brings an extensive background in communications, research and education, and international development work. Before joining the Center in late 1997, Mr. Brem was an independent consultant for nine years, working on social and economic issues for the Canadian International Development Agency (CIDA), private companies, charities, and UN organizations. He was communications director at the North-South Institute in Ottawa, Canada's leading think tank on developing countries and global issues. In that capacity he contributed to numerous studies and supervised some research projects while managing the publishing and information program. A former journalist, Mr. Brem served as editor-in-chief of nongovernmental organization (NGO) newspapers at international conferences on behalf of such groups as the International Coalition for Development Action, the International Organization of Consumers' Unions, and the UN Non-Governmental Liaison Service. He also worked on newspapers and magazines in Asia for seven years. Educated at basic level in New Zealand, he has an M.A. in political economy from the New

School for Social Research, New York City, and did postgraduate work in development studies at the State University of New York, Binghamton, and in Washington, D.C.

Christopher Pinney is director of the Imagine Program of the Canadian Centre for Philanthropy. Imagine is Canada's leading national program to promote corporate and public philanthropy. More than four hundred and fifty companies belong to Imagine's Caring Company Program. Mr. Pinney has worked in the private, public, and voluntary sectors and brings a combination of communication, advocacy, and community development experience to Imagine. He was director of communications for the Canadian Council for International Co-operation (CCIC), a coalition of more than one hundred and twenty Canadian voluntary organizations involved in international development. Mr. Pinney was executive director of the International Development Education Resources Centre; a senior partner with Westcoast Development Group, an economic development consulting firm based in Vancouver; and the western director for the National Film Board "Challenge for Change" program, a national community development initiative. He currently serves on the board of a number of voluntary agencies. Mr Pinney holds a B.A. in political science from McGill and an M.A. in communciations from Simon Fraser University.

Business Partners for Development: Vision, History, and Potential

4

Nigel Twose and Amanda Blakeley

The roles and responsibilities of business, civil society, and government have changed dramatically since the World Bank charter was drafted, and perhaps most dramatically in the past ten years. With the advent of globalization, the reduction in cost of telecommunications, the expansion of market economies throughout the world, and the collapse of the paternalistic state, the roles of the three sectors have become increasingly interdependent. We have moved from a world where the state had sole responsibility for the public good and business maximized profits independent of the interests of society at large to a world where success depends on the close synergy of interests among business, civil society, and government.

The private sector is the engine in wealth creation. It has also expanded widely to sectors previously considered public services, for example, from power and telephony to education and health. Today most companies accept that their long-term investment goals can only be achieved within stable social and financial environments; thus they are supporting a range of development activities. While not their core business, the success of these activities is essential to the success of their business. Increasingly, the business bottom line must be synchronized with the social bottom line for the communities in which the companies operate.

Civil society's role and influence is expanding. In the marketplace, the consumer has become "king." In the social arena, civil society has a growing influence on the behavior and governance of state, business, and individuals. Increasingly, civil society plays a key role in assessing the business community's contribution to the development arena, rewarding community friendly behavior and criticizing the opposite.

The public sector is having to reinvent itself. It is pulling out from the production of goods and the provision of services and is taking a more strategic approach to its role in society. Ideally, government's role is increasingly to foster the trust that creates social capital and mobilizes social forces and energy from all stakeholders.

The role of development organizations is rapidly changing to adapt to these new realities. To achieve poverty reduction, the ability of development institutions to affect the volume of private investment—both domestic and foreign—matters as much, if not more than how much money is lent to countries. In 1997 overseas development assistance (ODA) from Western governments totaled U.S.$37.3 billion; private sector flows to the developing world exceeded U.S.$256 billion (a sixfold rise from 1990). In this context, partnerships with the private sector can be an important strategy for poverty reduction, looking at and influencing the totality of a company's impact on society.

For the World Bank, this means a whole new agenda of working with governments to create an environment that will attract both domestic and foreign private investment in areas such as property rights, legal systems, guarantees, capital markets, and financial sector restructuring, among others. It means working with civil society—nongovernmental organizations (NGOs), foundations, and academic institutions—to help deliver development on the ground. It means working directly with business to maximize the development impact of resources flowing to developing countries, that is, helping to ensure that more is achieved with resources they are spending, and by increasing the effectiveness, encouraging them to spend more. The old order of the Bretton Woods institutions sitting on Mount Olympus and "doing development" from Washington is over. Partnerships with governments, civil society, private sector, and multilateral and bilateral donors, each playing to their respective strengths, is the only way forward.

THE GENESIS OF BUSINESS PARTNERS FOR DEVELOPMENT (BPD)

The Business Partners for Development (BPD) program has been in gestation for four years. The World Bank Group (WBG) began to explore the linkages between corporate social responsibility, social capital, and trisector partnerships in 1995 when British Petroleum came to the Bank looking for technical assistance in designing social programs in the Casanare region of Colombia. While this was an unprecedented role for the Bank to play, the Bank found that it was well positioned to play the role of neutral convenor, trusted by the business interests, government authorities, and civil society organizations active in the region.

At this same time, discussions began with the Prince of Wales Business Leaders Forum (PWBLF), which continues to provide strategic and intellectual leadership on matters of private sector partnerships for development. In

> ***"Increasingly, the business bottom line must be synchronized with the social bottom line for the communities in which the companies operate."***

1996–97 PWBLF received grant funding through the Development Grant Facility for the Business as Partners in Development research project. The project was designed to identify, analyze, and promote examples of business working in partnership with public sector institutions and NGOs to play a creative and positive role in the process of sustainable development. From this time on, the Bank was in its active "listening and learning" mode for two reasons. First, the Bank sought to determine if there was a role for it to play in promoting corporate citizenship; and secondly, if the answer was yes, to determine what to do to maximize the Bank's comparative advantages and minimize its weaknesses. This first phase culminated in an address to the Bank's board of executive directors, chaired by Jim Wolfensohn (the first instance where the Boardroom was opened to non-bank staffers), by five corporate CEOs and five heads of NGOs. Each of the speakers clearly said that the Bank group had a role to play in promoting corporate citizenship and partnerships, and told the assembly why their company or organization was involved and how it expected to benefit from the collaboration.

In response to the demand, the Finance and Private Sector Development Vice Presidency, headed by Jean-François Rischard, designed an initiative with interested partners within and outside the World Bank Group to facilitate strategic partnerships among business, civil society, and governments that build trust and more inclusive societies while benefiting the long-term interests of all three parties. The intent of this initiative was to focus with partners on aspirational standards of behavior, as opposed to designing codes of conduct. This was deliberately designed to avoid years of negotiation with corporate lawyers with the resulting code based on lowest common denominator compromises. Thus the initiative was formulated as an informal network of businesses, civil society organizations, and relevant government ministries, with the World Bank Group (WBG) as an equal partner. The core hypotheses were the following:

- Business partnerships for development provide win-win benefits to all three parties,
- Partnerships can be much more widely used throughout the world, and
- Partnerships can be scaled up to national and regional levels.

As originally conceived, the corporate citizenship initiative was structured around three interrelated campaigns:

1. Learning Campaign: to produce solid evidence of the positive impact of trisector partnerships—both the business benefits and the social and development benefits—and to prove the hypotheses mentioned above.
2. Action Campaign: to learn by doing; that is, demonstrating the impact by focusing on a set of pilot projects. At the core of partnership formation is the principle of social capital and building trust by working together. By developing specific projects, participants from the three sectors (business sector, civil society, and state) will acquire hands-on knowledge on how to build trust by working together strategically over a long-term period, for their own benefit and for that of the communities.
3. Sharing Campaign: to spread aggregate knowledge about effective partnerships and their potential contribution to development, through workshops, conferences, publications, knowledge banks, and a website.

BPD STRUCTURE

The World Bank convened a range of global firms and civil society organizations that were willing to share expertise and experience, devote resources, and work alongside governments and local community development organizations to further these three campaigns. Partners decided to spend three years working intensively with twelve to sixteen "focus projects" (that is, pilots) throughout the world and grouped into four "clusters." (The number of focus projects across all clusters is now close to thirty, because more partners have joined and proposed projects.) The first two clusters are formed along industry lines, because a critical mass of companies in these sectors had been working with the Bank and was interested in broadening and deepening their engagement in social development. The last two are theme-based groupings formed by initial key players who identified areas that would benefit from the trisector partnership approach. Each cluster designed its own specific objective and vision for the partnership:

1. *Natural Resources* (oil, gas, and mining companies): to develop guidelines/systems/structures for dealing with community issues and mitigating risk by optimizing development impact on host communities through trisector partnerships. Co-convenors: BP, CARE International, and the WBG.

2. *Water and Sanitation:* to identify specific lessons learned about partnerships from existing projects that are providing responsive and affordable water services to urban poor and to demonstrate that these can be replicated and scaled up to national and regional levels. Co-convenors: Générale des Eaux (Vivendi), WaterAid, and the WBG.
3. *Global Partnership for Youth Development:* to identify and share what works in building successful partnerships for youths, the next generation of laborers and consumers; then to create and work through existing national and global infrastructures to mobilize significant new resources to strengthen and scale up best practices in youth development. Co-convenors: the Kellogg Company, the International Youth Foundation, and the WBG. (Originally, we planned to have both a Youth Development and an Education and Training cluster. After initial difficulties in finding sponsorship for a separate Education and Training cluster idea, the two were merged. The Global Partnership for Youth Development now focuses broadly on four areas: education, vocational training for out-of-school youths, health and nutrition, and youth programs in the information technology sector.)
4. *Global Road Safety Partnership:* to reduce deaths, injuries, disabilities, and associated social costs of road traffic crashes through collaboration and coordination of road safety activities. Co-convenors: the International Federation of Red Cross and Red Crescent Societies and the WBG.

In June of 1998 what came to be known as the Business Partners for Development program received a U.S.$645,000 grant from the World Bank's Development Grant Facility (DGF) to seed the emerging initiative. This was the first year's tranche of WBG grant funding of an anticipated U.S.$3 million total for a three-year period. Operational costs of all focus projects are borne by the sponsoring companies, with few exceptions. Each cluster's budget is determined by aggregating the costs of the activities agreed by partners in relation to each focus project. Therefore, annual contributions differ across clusters. Direct financial and in-kind support to the clusters comes from the private sector partners, foundations, and governments as well as from the WBG (through grants, trust funds, adaptable lending instruments, and in a few cases, loans).

According to the DGF criteria, the seed grant can represent no more than 15 percent of the total program budget. Initially some questioned the seriousness of the Bank's commitment given this budgetary restriction; however, it is generally agreed that this serves to emphasize the point that the Bank is "an equal partner." Although the Bank initiated BPD and has devoted considerable staff time to the partnership, we have been clear that we are by no means leading or managing the initiative. Partners have carefully chosen a decentralized structure to guard against any one organization's domination and to ensure ownership by all partners.

Each of the clusters is co-convened by a multinational company, an international NGO, and the WBG, except in the case of the newest cluster. The Global Road Safety Partnership (GRSP) has only two co-convenors—an international NGO and the WBG—and a small steering committee with representation from all three sectors. Co-convenors are responsible for organizing the initial planning sessions to determine thematic focus, common objectives, and working methodology for the partnership; identifying, inviting, and actively working to secure partners for the cluster; making available operational staff to help build the partnership; helping ensure that the financial package is in place; participating in the governance of the partnership; and attending regular partnership meetings. The partnership funds are held by the co-convening NGO, which plays the role of secretariat. The BPD website is hosted by the World Bank's server, but each of the clusters is responsible for the content of its own website.

The World Bank, as a co-convenor of all four clusters, proposed a Knowledge Resource Group (KRG) to connect and collect lessons learned on trisector partnerships from all clusters, again to ensure that we are not the single repository and disseminator of cross-cutting knowledge. The KRG is co-convened by the WBG, the Prince of Wales Business Leaders Forum and CIVICUS, which also houses the secretariat. The KRG is not a fixed group, but is an association of individuals and organizations drawn from networks involved in trisector partnerships around the world. It is designed to be open and dynamic, combining the best available knowledge and experience. The KRG objective is to assist the process of collecting and connecting knowledge of trisector partnerships for human, social, and economic development such that practitioners become aware of, and try to improve on, what is being done elsewhere, maximizing the collective development impact of lessons learned. (See next chapter for more information.)

A basic BPD principle is the primacy of the clusters. Each cluster decides on and manages its own work program; no cluster or project is obliged to use KRG services or to maintain contact with other clusters. But each joint study visit needs facilitation; each training course needs trainers; all research needs researchers. Participants within each of the four clusters have good contacts with some specialists, and the KRG provides an additional, common available route to finding recommended and appropriate expertise available around the world. KRG's role is to make information about effective practices in trisector partnerships available, through the networks of those involved and particularly to the four clusters to assist their efforts to improve their partnerships.

BPD PHASES AND ACTIVITIES

The three-year time frame for BPD can be broken down into three nonsequential phases:

- Phase One: getting the elements in place for a work plan to be initiated (participants, projects, identification of priority partnership challenges and of BPD activity needs, establishment of a secretariat);
- Phase Two: implementing the work plan, centered on focus projects;
- Phase Three: aggregated learning, sharing, dissemination, and promotion.

The Natural Resources, Water and Sanitation, and Youth Development clusters have now completed phase one. The Road Safety cluster was only formally launched in February 1999, yet it has almost completed phase one. Phase two will involve the following cluster activities as identified through needs assessments performed by each of the focus projects:

- Joint study visits, with participants from the three sectors in other focus projects coming together in one site to explore common solutions to agreed partnership challenges;
- Workshops at a national level exploring other trisector partnership experience in that country, and opportunities for replication and scale up;
- Research on commonly identified challenges;
- Training to fill identified expertise gaps;
- Monitoring and evaluation of projects.

The starting point when convening BPD partners and potential partners has been to clearly state each organization's interest in joining such a network along with desired outcomes. For the World Bank Group, our objective is to influence the way we do business, that is, to mainstream the trisector partnership approach throughout our lending and investment activities. This is facilitated by increasing colleagues' exposure to and involvement in BPD activities and processes. Participation in BPD represents a fantastic learning opportunity, in terms of learning both from the focus projects and from the experience of partners. Along with stating each partner's objectives, it has been necessary to state the comparative advantage of each in joining BPD. Partnership entails shared responsibility and distinct accountabilities for achieving the objectives of all players.

Support for BPD has been growing steadily since Jim Wolfensohn held a press conference alongside corporate and civil society representatives to officially launch the network at the World Bank's 1998 annual meetings. Moreover, the World Bank Group is being asked increasingly to engage more substantively with the private sector beyond lending and donor-based relationships. We are in discussion with a variety of units throughout the Bank, each of which brings a consortium of interested business and civil society partners, to expand the BPD approach. The following areas are being discussed as possible BPD-style clusters: HIV/AIDS, disaster mitigation, sustainable cities, financial services and small and midsized enterprises (SMEs), business development, and a regionally based initiative for Africa.

CHALLENGES AND LESSONS LEARNED

Over the course of BPD's development, we have learned several important lessons in partnership formation, many of them stemming from tensions and delays. The first one is that this type of decentralized, informal network will only work if it is demand driven and not buoyed by the interests of individual partners. We learned this lesson after struggling to develop an education cluster without partner, notably corporate, support.

The second lesson is more of a reflection on the natural process of partnership development. BPD has taken a long time to build and grow. Partnerships are likely to involve a range of interrelated activities over time, steadily building consensus and ownership within each institution involved in the partnership and among its stakeholders. Such relationships require a level of mutual trust and respect and a clear understanding of each other's strengths and weaknesses. This process takes time, and we have been clear from the outset that the up-front transaction costs for each partner will be greater than if each decided to go it alone, with the anticipated long-term benefits expected to outweigh those that would accrue from flying solo. We have, however, learned institutional lessons to facilitate and encourage partnerships and are in the process of trying to gain approval inside the World Bank. Mechanisms and tools being developed to support partnerships include a private sector partnership strategy, guidelines for engaging with the private sector, an easily accessible and updateable database of all partnerships, a tool kit to ease the burden on World Bank staff members engaging in partnerships, and in-house training programs on

> *"Increasingly, civil society plays a key role in assessing the business community's contribution to the development arena, rewarding community friendly behavior and criticizing the opposite."*

partnerships. Ideally, World Bank staff members and partners will not have to re-create the wheel each time they engage in partnership.

The third lesson is the challenge and occasional tension arising from "complementary" versus "common" objectives of BPD partners. For the World Bank, all our work and initiatives must be designed to further our mission of poverty reduction. Private sector partners are typically interested in the business benefits that will accrue from their participation in BPD. An example of this is the tensions that sometimes arise between BPD's learning agenda and the focus project sponsors' strong desire to see practical improvements in their projects. While these dual objectives are not mutually exclusive, there is often a fine line connecting the two. Partners have learned that extra efforts must be expended to design activities in such a way that they bridge this gap and sit at the nexus of varying objectives. The BPD process has shown us that this point can be reached, but again it may entail increased up-front transaction costs. These costs can be minimized by expending the effort early in the partnership to clearly state each partner's objectives, comparative advantages, and constraints, and to work toward aggregating them into a coherent joint strategy for the partnership.

Closely correlated to this lesson is the recognized need to define each partner's role. Tensions inevitably arise in the struggle between planning and laying the foundation of the partnership and action and implementation of the agreed activities. Experience suggests that the extra time it takes to lay the groundwork and define each other's respective and complementary roles pays dividends to all partners and avoids confusion and miscommunication at later stages. All partners, especially those from the private sector, are eager to move from conceptualizing to implementation as early as possible. As mentioned earlier, new mechanisms are in design to facilitate this process without ignoring the structural needs of the partnership.

Finally, there is a clear need to scale up this approach and to spread the learning throughout the World Bank Group. We have learned the importance of internal champions and supporters, in our case from relevant technical and regional units throughout the Bank, to ensure the necessary momentum and ownership. The greatest challenge we faced in this area has been with the Global Partnership for Youth Development, owing to the fact that the World Bank does not have a youth development unit (youth issues are dealt with across the education, health, population, nutrition, and social protection departments). Therefore, this cluster has, until recently, been supported on the Bank's side mainly from the centralized BPD team and the relevant country departments. The Bank's Human Development Department is currently in the process of drafting the Bank's first youth strategy and convening a thematic group on youths. This is one example of how BPD learning is spreading into the policies of the institution. We also recognize the need to mainstream the trisector partnership approach throughout our business line; that is, to have partnerships be a recognized component in our lending and investing activities.

Nigel Twose is senior partnerships specialist, working with the World Bank's vice president for private sector development and infrastrucure. He is responsible for formulating the World Bank Group's private sector partnership strategy. He initiated and has management responsibility for the Business Partners for Development network and leads Bank strategy on corporate social responsibility. Before joining the World Bank in 1997, Mr. Twose had a 21-year career with nongovernmental organizations, including postings in West Africa and Nepal. Most recently, he worked as program director for the British NGO ActionAid, where he oversaw the development of a wide range of business partnerships. Mr. Twose has written widely on development issues.

Amanda Blakeley has worked on private sector partnerships with the World Bank's vice president for private sector development and infrastructure since July 1995. She works primarily on the Business Partners for Development program. Ms. Blakeley helped initiate the program, manages the Bank's participation in the Global Partnership for Youth Development, developed a BPD toolkit, and is responsible for exploring new partnerships. Before joining the World Bank in 1995, Ms. Blakeley started her own small business in California and most recently worked as an associate for Trinity International Partners in Washington, D.C. Ms. Blakeley received her undergraduate degree in political science from Stanford University and a master's degree in international relations and international economics from Johns Hopkins School of Advanced International Studies (SAIS).

The Learning and Sharing Process: Why Is Partnership between Sectors such a Challenge?

5

Ros Tennyson and Alina Zyszkowski

Working cross-sectorally is undoubtedly a challenging experience. Most who have tried it have been shocked at how much time and effort has been needed to set up, develop, and sustain partnerships. Some have given up because they simply have not had the confidence or skills to meet the challenges head on. Others have persevered—often in isolation—only to find that the external circumstances have changed around them and the partnerships have unraveled. Only a few partnerships in different parts of the world (for example, Philippine Business for Social Progress in Manila) have survived the test of time and provide us with some living examples of how good it can be when it works.

Apart from the problems of forming the partnership in the first place, there is the additional fact that partnerships can be slow to "deliver." They are not a "quick fix" solution to serious development issues. Most of us are impatient. Many situations are desperate. Can we wait for partnerships to provide solutions?

Everyone involved (or potentially involved) in partnerships for sustainable development has good reason to be sceptical. Each sector has its history suggesting that it is not very good at collaboration. This can be understood as the natural outcome of particular sector characteristics:

- Business *is* profit focused and competitive,
- The public sector *is* bureaucratic and inflexible, and
- The nongovernmental organization (NGO) sector *is* territorial and combative.

Whichever sector you come from, do not let go of your scepticism until you have tried and tested the model and you find for yourself that partnership really does add value to what you aim to achieve.

We should not, in any case, assume that partnerships are *de facto* a good thing. "Partnership" happens to be the buzzword of the new millennium but does that make it the "right" strategy?

> ***"Most who have tried them have been shocked at how much time and effort has been needed to set up, develop, and sustain partnerships."***

Perhaps the only thing we can say with confidence is that partnerships are definitely worth a try. Where aid and trade have failed to provide long-term, sustainable solutions, there is a hope that genuine collaboration (based on principles of equity and mutual benefit) can provide locally appropriate and locally sustainable solutions.

But to really develop a systematic partnership approach to development and to scale up such approaches when they are found to work, some fast and serious learning has to take place.

WHAT KINDS OF "LEARNING" CAN HELP PARTNERSHIPS WORK WELL?

Perhaps the most obvious "learning" is learning to be tolerant. Prejudice and preconceptions are not the best basis for collaboration—but how do you start the process of engaging and bridge building with people you have, until now, at best misunderstood and, at worst, hated? What we have attempted to summarize below are some of the key "learnings" that need to be developed. This is based on experience over many years that has been reinforced and clearly articulated by the more recent Business Partners for Development (BPD) experience. It should be noted that this "learnings" check list is applicable to people from *any* sector—the first steps toward brokering and nurturing a partnership can come from *anyone.*

DEVELOPING A PARTNERSHIP "LEARNING" CHECK LIST

1. Learning New Professional Skills

- Active listening—developing sincere interest in what others have to say to genuinely understand what they can contribute and "bring to the table."
- Open communication—being honest and "up front" about

what each partner wants and expects from the partnership and what is (and is not) working.

- Mediation and negotiation—recognizing that compromise does not have to mean "selling out."

2. Learning from Experience

- Getting "inside" each other's organizational values—for example, by spending a day in a business partner's factory, at the local government office, or with an NGO working in the community.
- Going to see successful partnerships in action and asking lots of penetrating questions.
- Trying it out yourself; making mistakes and learning from them.

3. Learning How to Use Language as a Partnership-Building Tool

Partners need to recognize the differences in language usage. On the one hand, this is learning how to cut through sector "jargon." On the other hand, it means learning how to use language more precisely and sensitively.

For example, the word "profit" (which makes partnerships with business so difficult for the public sector and NGOs) in its original definition actually means "benefit" according to the *Oxford English Dictionary.* Only some sectors are concerned with profit (in the sense of personal financial gain) but *all* sectors are concerned with "benefit"—a simple substitute of one word for another gives instant common ground.

Similarly, people trying to build partnerships often talk about finding "common" goals. In reality this is impossible. Goals are inevitably different and, one could argue, so they should be. Perhaps it is "complementary" goals rather than "common" goals that are more realistic and achievable (and appropriate?).

In the same vein, in a partnership is one truly wanting only to "measure impact" (outdated "donor-speak") or more usefully also wanting to "assess value"? Moving from the "impact" on "beneficiaries" to an assessment of "value" to all "stakeholders" changes the nature of the discussion and partnership substantially, and for the better.

4. Learning to Be Imaginative

Creating new collaborative relationships requires imagination as well as stamina. The most enduring partnerships are often those that have taken risks and that have tried the unexpected. Either allow your (and your partners') latent cre-

> *"Similarly, people trying to build partnerships often talk about finding 'common' goals. In reality this is impossible. Goals are inevitably different and, one could argue, so they should be. Perhaps it is 'complementary' goals rather than 'common' goals that are more realistic and achievable (and appropriate?)."*

ativity to flourish or bring in those who can inspire a dynamic and imaginative approach. An important ingredient to a successful partnership is the ability to creatively engage each other as you share new and "outside the box" ideas.

5. Learning How to Prove It Works

If you become a converted sceptic because you try a partnership approach and find it is successful, then see yourself as a "practitioner researcher" and develop your own action research initiatives that are stakeholder based and that provide convincing evidence of success. Then learn some new communications skills to convince others (for example, your still-sceptical colleagues, potential new partners, cynical stakeholders, current and future donors, the general public, politicians, and the media).

6. Learning What Does Not Work

Learn to become a "critical practitioner." Partnerships need common sense, not euphoria. Analyze what goes wrong so you understand why it went wrong and adjust your practice accordingly. Why did a specific company or NGO or public sector agency refuse to join a partnership? Why did the balance of power in a partnership become unequal? Why did a partnership not achieve the goals it set? (Note: If your experience to date has yielded evidence of what does *not* work in partnerships, it would be helpful to let us know—especially if you think this points out a general principle or rule that may have universal applicability.)

Keep reminding yourself that partnership may *not* be the answer to every development issue or opportunity. Learn to assess which issues will be well served by a partnership approach and which issues are better dealt with by a single sector.

WHAT CAN USEFULLY BE SHARED BETWEEN PRACTITIONERS?

We use the term partnership "practitioner" to mean anyone, anywhere who has a role in building or managing cross-sector partnerships—whether at a small-scale, local level or at an international, strategic level and whatever their sector background. The number of such practitioners grows daily and networks are developing to provide linkages that offer a mixture of experience exchange and support systems.

But what exactly is it that can truly be shared between practitioners? Is it models or methods?

Experience suggests that it is unusual for a model of partnership to be directly transported from one setting to another. Successful models can, however, do two other things. They can:

- Build confidence about what is possible, and
- Share partnership-building processes and identify the key success factors that have made the partnership work.

While models of specific partnership projects are rarely successfully replicated, methods of partnership building are proving to be surprisingly universal.

HOW HAS THE BUSINESS PARTNERS FOR DEVELOPMENT PROGRAM ENGAGED IN THE LEARNING PROCESS?

As mentioned in the previous chapter, the Business Partners for Development program has identified the need to learn from and share partnership experiences. A specific cross-program cluster has been established and is known as the Knowledge Resource Group (KRG). KRG is an international network of individuals and organizations that have particular and in-depth experience in partnerships among the three sectors (government, business, and civil society) and that are willing to share that experience with others.

The KRG is co-convened by three organizations—broadly representing a sector "constituency." These organizations are CIVICUS (civil society), the Prince of Wales Business Leaders Forum (BLF) (private sector), and the World Bank Group (public sector). Thus the KRG itself is a partnership of organizations with complementary, if not necessarily common, goals. Learning how to work together and in creative and dynamic relationship with each other and the rest of the BPD "system" has already taken about a year. This is not a surprise. Partnership building—as we have implied throughout—is a slow process.

> *"Where aid and trade have failed to provide long-term, sustainable solutions, there is a hope that genuine collaboration (based on principles of equity and mutual benefit) can provide locally appropriate and locally sustainable solutions."*

Like the other BPD clusters, where the secretariat for the cluster is housed within a nongovernmental organization, the KRG secretariat is based at CIVICUS. It undertakes three coordination functions, which provide:

- A communications channel for BPD as a whole and with a large number of other and external audiences;
- A single point of contact for inquiries, technical service providers, and the development of tools and "products" based on the BPD experience; and
- Support for BPD in terms of coordinating and planning general meetings and workshops to gather lessons learned and to share effective tools as well as providing access to a consultative group that offers its specialist advice from its international experience.

Specifically, the secretariat is building a database of specialists who have a proven track record in cross-sector partnership work as facilitators, brokers, or researchers; a website with information about BPD and its learnings and linkages; and a basic communications and dissemination infrastructure.

In addition to these services, the KRG is developing a range of specialist programs and products that are used (and, in effect, pilot tested) by the clusters before being revised and disseminated more widely. These action learning materials include a comprehensive set of "tools" for organizers, host organizations, and facilitators involved in the development and management of partnership study visits.

WHERE THE WORK OF THE KRG CAN ADD VALUE TO PARTNERSHIPS WITHIN BPD AND BEYOND

It is the role of KRG to:

- Connect with the practitioners and specialists worldwide who are working on trisector partnerships,
- Provide a conduit for lessons learned (knowledge) to and from the clusters as they work to develop their focus projects,

- Observe the process and reflect on the common patterns and diversity between clusters,
- Respond to requests for information or help from the growing BPD network,
- Document the complexity of BPD through all its development phases (and growing pains),
- Extract the elements of the program that are truly innovative and of wider application and value, and
- Disseminate experience as widely and vividly as possible.

Dissemination of the BPD experience is critical. The program has many points of originality and innovation and is working with a wide range of focus projects of both large and small scale all over the world. The cross-cultural nature of these trisector partnerships is a special point of interest. Observing, analyzing, recording, contributing to and communicating the BPD experience are important and demanding tasks.

The fact that a wide range of partners from the different sectors and from all over the world meet and talk to each other is in itself an exciting result of BPD. This achievement should not be underestimated because in many cases there has been little or no previous contact or interaction among the sectors. For all those involved in BPD, their way of approaching their work and "doing business" will never be quite the same again.

The KRG works as a catalyst and facilitator, using the BPD experience to promote change in the World Bank, in multinational corporations and business organizations, and in civil society at all levels, from international NGOs to small community groups. The partnerships linked to BPD are dynamic and constantly evolving, as is the learning process generated from these partnerships. KRG seeks, on behalf of BPD as a whole, to capture that dynamic element and institutionalize it within each sector.

KRG is supporting—and studying—the transformational processes involved in successful partnerships. The underlying assumption of all its work is that long-term change only occurs through the interaction of different players working together on a clear and shared development task. What we all want to know at the end of this process is—what exactly is the "value added" from these partnerships? How does each sector constituency view this added value? The KRG's task is to answer such questions, so it looks for:

- Evidence of transformed attitudes, behavior, and results;
- New ideas and initiatives that can inspire others;
- Ways to improve or scale up existing partnerships;
- Ways to facilitate the process of building and sustaining partnerships through freely sharing time-saving techniques and other

tools that help partnership practitioners get to the heart of issues rapidly and effectively;

- Ways to learn lessons from others, with a particular interest in cross-cultural learning;
- The right tools to develop that will build skills and confidence; and
- Effective ways to develop strategic networks based on shared learning.

SOME FINAL THOUGHTS ON LEARNING AND SHARING

Our final word on the subject of learning and sharing is that this is ultimately and essentially about "doing." Actions speak louder than words. Learning and sharing is about helping new partnerships come into being and making existing partnerships work better.

Ros Tennyson comes from an NGO background and has worked with the Prince of Wales Business Leaders Forum (BLF) for the past eight years, leading the Forum's cutting-edge work on cross-sector partnership building. She is the author of "Managing Partnerships—Tools for Mobilising the Public Sector, Business, and Civil Society," which was funded by business and is now in general circulation in all three sectors. Ms. Tennyson is a senior development adviser to the BLF and the director of the Resource Centre for Socially Responsible Business Practice, which is funded by the U.K.'s Department for International Development. She is a co-convenor of BPD's Knowledge Resources Group with CIVICUS and the World Bank and is currently working on a training manual for partnership "brokers" in collaboration with the United Nations Staff College.

Alina Zyszkowski is coordinator for the Knowledge Resource Group (KRG) Secretariat of the Business Partners for Development project. CIVICUS serves as host for the KRG secretariat and is a co-convenor of the KRG along with the Prince of Wales Business Leaders Forum and the World Bank Group. She has worked in the nonprofit sector for more than ten years, including experience with several international NGOs. She has a Master's Degree in Social Work from The Catholic University of America and a Bachelor's Degree of Arts in International Studies from The Johns Hopkins University. She edited "Small Islands, Big Issues."

For more information about Business Partners for Development and the Knowledge Resource Group: <http://www.worldbank.org/bpd>; also available through <http://www.civicus.org>. If you have partnership experiences of value to share with others in the form of succinct and well-structured case studies, send them to us so we can add them to our collection and use them to amplify the partnership-building work of others.

KRG Secretariat, CIVICUS, 919 18th Street, NW, Third Floor, Washington, DC 20006, U.S.A. (Telephone +1-202-331-8518, Fax +1-202-331-8774, E-mail: krgsecretariat@civicus.org.)

Copies of the action learning materials for conducting successful study visits are available from The Prince of Wales Business Leaders Forum, 15–16 Cornwell Terrace, Regent's Park, London NWI 4QP, U.K. (Telephone +44-171-467-3656, Fax: +44-171-467-3610, www.oneworld.org/pwblf)

Capturing the Lessons of Partnership and Practice: A Review of Corporate-NGO Partnerships in Asia Pacific

6

Tadashi Yamamoto

PREFACE

There was an air of excitement in the room, as some eighty representatives of corporations and civil society organizations from countries mainly in the Asia Pacific region gathered in Tokyo in June 1999 to discuss emerging patterns of corporate-NGO (nongovernmental organization) partnership. The meeting, organized by the Japan Center for International Exchange (JCIE) in cooperation with Keidanren (Federation of Economic Organizations), the Council for Better Corporate Citizenship (CBCC), the One-Percent Club, and the Asia Pacific Philanthropy Consortium (APPC), focused on a set of eleven case studies on corporate-NGO partnerships in the Asia Pacific region that were undertaken by JCIE. (The results of the case studies will be published by JCIE under the title *Corporate-NGO Partnership in Asia Pacific*. Complete versions of the original case studies will also be made available on the JCIE website <http://www.jcie.or.jp>.)

These eleven cases, which were presented at the conference, in most cases by individuals who had been involved in the partnerships themselves, were quite diverse in terms of the national origin of corporations, business sector, and NGO partners. A number of corporations not covered in the case studies were also represented at the conference, and they shared their experiences as well. What emerged from this meeting and the case studies, and what generated excitement among the participants, seems to be a new impetus for the development of both civil society and corporate philanthropy, which have been gaining momentum in the region in recent years.

The Tokyo conference took place at a time when most Asian nations were still going through the traumatic process of recovering from a financial crisis that has beset the region since July 1997.

That crisis dramatically reversed the euphoric atmosphere that prevailed in the region until just a few years ago, inspired by the phenomenal economic growth that was dubbed the "East Asian Miracle." Although the circumstances were quite different when the case studies project was conceived, the initial premise of the project—that corporate-NGO partnership is gaining importance in the Asia Pacific region—proved to be even more relevant as the project progressed. The exploration of such questions as why partnerships are beneficial, how to forge partnerships, and how to manage effective partnerships has assumed sharper focus and added urgency as a result of the financial crisis. Although the case studies and discussion at the Tokyo conference did not provide clear-cut answers to all of these questions, they deepened our understanding of the nature of corporate-NGO partnership and the challenges of bringing about successful partnership arrangements.

EVOLVING ASIA PACIFIC REGIONAL CONTEXT OF CORPORATE-NGO PARTNERSHIP

Impact of the Evolving Context on Civil Society

It is clear that the remarkable economic development of the past decades contributed greatly to the growth of civil society in Asia, touching off forces of democratization and social change. Many Asian NGOs, which were established in the latter part of the 1980s and the early part of the 1990s, were formed primarily by individuals from the emerging middle class who could articulate the general public's concern for such issues as the environment, human rights, and inequality.

Conversely, the negative consequences of rapid economic development in the region have contributed equally to the rise of civil society in Asia. NGOs claim that Asian governments have not been able to bring about equitable economic development, and that it is therefore the responsibility of the nongovernmental sector to come up with alternative policies that can offer a more equitable distribution of the benefits of economic growth.

The financial crisis in Asia has clearly had a major impact on the region's NGOs, presenting them with greater challenges than ever before. As economic conditions have worsened and the human impact has become evident in many areas, the expectations placed on civil society have grown. Many governments have been pressed to downsize drastically and reduce their budget allocation for dealing with the crisis, which has left civil society to fill the void.

Most important, the financial crisis has served to broaden the debate over the role of civil society organizations in these Asian countries. There has been growing public acceptance of the idea that civil society organizations are forces of sociopolitical and economic reform that can contribute to improve-

"It is clear that the remarkable economic development of the past decades contributed greatly to the growth of civil society in Asia, touching off forces of democratization and social change. . . . Conversely, the negative consequences of rapid economic development in the region have contributed equally to the rise of civil society in Asia."

ments in the governance of society. The deficiency of governance in many of these countries has come to the fore as the crisis, to a great extent, has been attributed to the absence of transparency and accountability in Asian governments.

Impact of the Evolving Context on Corporate Philanthropy

When Asian countries were going through periods of phenomenal economic gains, a growing number of corporations, both indigenous and foreign, were increasing their support for efforts to address social needs. As corporations endeavored to grow and sustain new markets in Asia, they were frequently confronted with social, legal, and economic conditions that affected the production and sale of their products and services. These conditions often resulted in a greater appreciation for the relationship between corporate self-interest and the health of communities.

As corporate activities continued to expand their role as engines of economic growth in Asia Pacific countries, their impact on society became stronger. There was a growing trend for corporations to depart from traditional patterns of charitable giving for the poor and the needy and to engage more actively and directly in dealing with social problems.

The financial crisis has had contradictory effects on corporate philanthropy in the region. On the one hand, as many businesses have faltered or collapsed, it has decreased the ability of corporations to give. On the other hand, as the needs of society have increased, corporations have faced increasing demands for assistance. Moreover, there is an added pressure on corporations to contribute to the development of viable communities and sustainable markets because many believe it was their arcane systems of corporate governance, such as collusive relations between corporate officers and government bureaucrats, that contributed to the economic debacle in the region.

Impact of the Evolving Context on Corporate-NGO Partnerships

Most of the countries in Asia that achieved the "East Asian Miracle" had a system of governance that was well suited to pursue the single purpose of rapid economic growth. Governments were considered to be the sole arbiter of public goods during that period, and corporations as well as civil society organizations were put under their control or guidance. These traditional systems of governance, which worked well for many years, have been shaken by forces of globalization that have created complex social issues requiring fundamental domestic adjustments. It has become quite obvious that many of the region's governments can no longer cope with such rapidly growing social needs, thus leaving a widening space for new actors from the NGO and corporate sectors.

The case studies and discussion at the Tokyo conference reinforced the premise of the project that the evolving environment in Asia is particularly conducive to partnership in that the problems facing society are increasingly complex and interconnected. Finding solutions will require multiple sources of talent, resources, and expertise, drawing on attributes found within all sectors of society. When based on the respective strengths of those involved, these partnerships can extend the benefits of each partner's resources, dignify and empower all parties involved, and amplify the impact of their efforts.

WHY PARTNERSHIP? BUSINESS AND CIVIL SOCIETY PERSPECTIVES

Business Perspectives

All of the cases taken up in the Corporate-NGO Partnership Project demonstrate the increasing attention that corporations give to the health of the communities where they operate. Corporations have found working with local NGOs, which respond to needs of stakeholders in the communities, to be of benefit to the corporations themselves. One particular quality that corporations are able to make use of is the reputation and credibility of certain NGOs in the communities. Corporations choose NGO partners that represent certain values and concerns of the community. NGOs also offer corporate partners specialized professional expertise to respond to the needs of the communities into which corporations wish to move. Some corporations even hold the view that fostering the development of capable NGOs as agents for change in the communities will serve their own long-term interest.

Certain practical motivations for corporations seeking NGO partners were also discussed at the Tokyo conference. In the face of growing competition, enhancing the corporate image through substantive contributions to soci-

"It should be noted that corporate-NGO partnerships generally operate within broader multisectoral partnerships, involving governments, intellectual leaders, the media, and members of the community. It is especially important to recognize the role of the public sector, as it continues to play a vital function in serving the public interest and in providing an enabling environment for the corporate-NGO partnership."

ety has become an essential factor for improved corporate performance. More fundamentally, a growing number of corporations view partnership with NGOs as a part of establishing their own identity in society and improving their corporate governance.

In his keynote speech at the Tokyo conference, Yotaro Kobayashi, chairman of Fuji-Xerox Corporation and chairman of the Japan Association of Corporate Executives, noted that profitmaking is the most important means by which his company tries to achieve its founding objectives, but it is by no means the ultimate objective. Corporations, however, are under pressure from two sides: on the one hand, there is pressure to be more productive and profitable; while on the other hand, there is pressure from the stakeholders to be more viable in a broader societal perspective. He emphasized that balancing these two requirements is part of the very important agenda that new systems of corporate governance should address. He added that partnership with NGOs seems to be an appropriate means to strike this balance. Several corporations analyzed in the case studies project underscored Kobayashi's view, having expressed a clear commitment to partnership with NGOs as part of their corporate philosophies.

NGO Perspectives

The increasing attention being given by NGOs to partnerships with corporations is based, in the first instance, on their interest in capital mobilization in the form of either cash or gifts-in-kind. Such corporate support has become important in part because of the dwindling availability of public funding that has resulted from the budget constraints facing many governments. It should be noted, however, that NGOs also seek corporate financial contributions to diversify and multiply their sources of funding to avoid the government control that can result from exclusive reliance on public funding.

Second, NGOs are interested in partnership arrangements as corporations are increasingly willing to provide human resources through corporate volunteer activities. This type of contribution is extremely important to the viable operation of NGOs, which often lack management and administrative know-how. The transfer of skills in such areas as financial management, strategic planning, and information technology is therefore essential in building a stronger institutional infrastructure for NGOs. Marketing skills are also an important contribution that corporations can offer, since many NGOs provide services to citizens or earn income through sales of their products and services. As indicated in several case studies, an increasing number of NGOs are becoming business-like, and partnership with corporations is a powerful instrument for NGOs seeking to develop a self-sustaining pattern of activities.

Third, corporations bring to the partnership a sense of accountability and a hard-nosed, result-oriented attitude often lacking in their NGO counterparts.

REQUIREMENTS FOR EFFECTIVE CORPORATE-NGO PARTNERSHIP

Kumi Naidoo, secretary general of CIVICUS, captured the essence of the Corporate-NGO Partnership Project case studies in a list of keywords that he offered in his keynote speech at the Tokyo conference. Crystallized in "Kumi's six principles" are the building blocks of effective partnerships: (1) clarity of vision and purpose, (2) constant self-regulation, (3) commitment, (4) communication, (5) consistency, and (6) change management. These principles closely coincide with the key findings that this author presented in a draft overview of the case studies report.

First and foremost, as is evident from the preceding section, the commitment of corporations to the health of communities is a fundamental prerequisite for an effective partnership with NGOs. The case studies underscored that a clear statement by corporate leaders of commitment to the community is crucial for the successful realization of partnerships with NGOs. Moreover, such a commitment and philosophy must be institutionalized within the company through effective communication efforts throughout the corporation, in appropriate corporate channels, and, even more important, through the involvement of employees in the implementation of partnerships with NGOs.

Identifying an appropriate partner NGO that is well established and accepted in the community where corporations are operating—and that is equipped with appropriate skills to respond to the needs of the community—is clearly another prerequisite for effective partnership arrangements. Several

> *"There has been growing public acceptance of the idea that civil society organizations are forces of sociopolitical and economic reform that can contribute to improvements in the governance of society."*

cases also emphasized that corporations have to be flexible in applying their guidelines to localize their community involvement activities appropriately.

Finally, in building these partnerships, most cases pointed to the importance of intermediaries that can bring together corporations and NGOs and facilitate their working relationships. Such an intermediary function is particularly important when corporations move into different sociocultural settings, or when they are entering new fields.

CONCLUSIONS

Given the limited sampling included in the case studies, it is difficult to form any definitive conclusions about the scope and utility of corporate-NGO partnerships in the Asia Pacific region. However, some very general conclusions may be drawn from the case studies and the Tokyo conference discussion. Although the number of corporate-NGO partnerships may still be limited in the Asia Pacific region, there clearly is an indication of their growing importance. The changing context in the region clearly favors further development of partnerships, and there is increasing interest among corporations and NGOs in such arrangements.

A second conclusion is that corporate-NGO partnerships take diverse patterns, and thus there is no simple model for success. There are certain criteria, however, that should be taken into account in bringing about the partnership, as discussed above.

Third, it should be noted that corporate-NGO partnerships generally operate within broader multisectoral partnerships, involving governments, intellectual leaders, the media, and members of the community. It is especially important to recognize the role of the public sector, as it continues to play a vital function in serving the public interest and in providing an enabling environment for the corporate-NGO partnership.

Fourth, corporate-NGO partnerships cannot be promoted as long as the traditional attitude of "us against them" remains between corporations and NGOs. Efforts are needed to further dismantle the lingering lack of trust between the two sectors. There are encouraging signs that these exclusionary attitudes on both sides are beginning to break down. As evidenced by the Tokyo conference participants, a new breed of corporate manager is emerging that has had some experience working with NGOs as a student or corporate volunteer, and, conversely, an increasing number of NGO leaders have corporate backgrounds.

Finally, the Case Studies Project and the Tokyo conference discussion reinforced a strong belief held by the multinational group of researchers who worked together on the project that partnership of any kind depends in the final analysis on people who see the importance, value, and joy in working together. Several participants in the Tokyo conference emphasized that more forums are needed where people from corporations and NGOs can come together to improve their mutual understanding and share common aspirations to promote more effective corporate-NGO partnerships in the Asia Pacific region. We hope the Corporate-NGO Partnership Project and its final report enhance such sharing and dialogue between the two sectors.

Tadashi Yamamoto is president of the Japan Center for International Exchange (JCIE), which he founded in 1970. Under his leadership, JCIE, through its Global ThinkNet, CivilNet, and Political Exchange programs, has been working to strengthen Japan's role in international policy dialogue and cooperation networks. He currently is a member as well as the Japanese director of the Trilateral Commission, the U.K.-Japan 2000 Group, the Japanese-German Dialogue Forum, and the Korea-Japan Forum, and is a member of the Korea-Japan Joint Committee for Promoting History Studies. He also serves as member of the board of the Asian Community Trust and of the Japan NPO Center. He was appointed a member and coordinator of the Prime Minister's Commission on Japan's Goals in the 21st Century. Mr. Yamamoto studied at Sophia University, continued his education in the United States at St. Norbert College, and received his M.B.A. from Marquette University in Wisconsin. He is editor or author of several books on civil society and the nonprofit sector, including "Nonprofit Sector in Japan," "Deciding the Public Good," "Emerging Civil Society in the Asia Pacific Community," and "The Corporate-NGO Partnership in Asia Pacific."

Capturing the Lessons of Partnership and Practice: Initiatives to Promote Corporate Engagement in Latin America

7

Marisol Pagés and Nelson Stratta[1]

As the century draws to a close, Latin America is in the midst of consolidating democratic institutions and rising to the challenges of globalization. Economically, the region has remained on a path of moderate growth and stable prices throughout the latter 1990s, reversing the ravaging trends of economic stagnation and hyperinflation that characterized it during the "lost decade" of the 1980s. Furthermore, economic integration at the subregional and hemispheric levels is rapidly gaining ground. Politically, most countries of the region are headed by democratically elected governments and are undergoing profound decentralization processes. Significant reforms to legal and judicial systems are under way to allow for more participatory and just societies.

CHALLENGES TO PARTNERSHIPS

The magnitude of these changes presents great challenges to Latin America. Despite the region's significant democratic advances and economic achievements, counteracting trends point to the frailty of its young democracies and markets. In most countries underlying patterns of unequal distribution continue to be exacerbated and social problems have deepened as a result of austere economic reforms and reduced state social expenditures. The region has one of the worst income distributions in the world, with the richest 20 percent of the population receiving approximately twenty times more income than the poorest 20 percent and at least one-quarter of the population

[1] The authors would like to acknowledge the research undertaken by the Chilean Benchmarking Group, Fundacion Esquel Ecuador, Fundacao Grupo Esquel Brasil, the Inter-American Democracy Network, the Inter-American Foundation, and the Representatives in Latin America of the Prince of Wales Business Leaders Forum, which forms the basis of this analysis.

living below the poverty line.[2] As expressed by Enrique Iglesias, president of the Inter-American Development Bank, "Latin America has contracted an enormous social debt with its inhabitants which originated in its historical heritage and has not been attended to by the failed development strategies of the last decades . . . and has been magnified by the crisis and adjustment programs of the 1980s."[3] Recent events, such as the ravaging effects of large terrorist organizations in Colombia, the concentration of power by Peru's Alberto Fujimori, and the attempted *coup d'état* in Paraguay, among others, also point to potential breakdowns in the rule of law within nominally democratic systems. In the context of an historically nonparticipatory culture inherited from colonial systems of government and a crisis of traditional political parties, citizen discord has few outlets. Thus the persistent increases in drug use and criminal violence being experienced by most Latin American countries could be interpreted, in large part, as manifestations of these unvented economic and social frustrations. These enduring problems challenge the long-term sustainability of political and macroeconomic stability and make evident the need for a collaborative approach to development in the region.

The spaces occupied but now being vacated by the once omnipresent public sector in Latin America are increasingly being filled by a complex web of actors—many times in association—including local and regional governments; local, regional, and international civil society organizations; and the domestic and international private sector. Civil society has become an active player in the national development arena, particularly for its ability to deliver social services effectively to marginalized populations and incrementally for its contributions to the policy debate. In addition, there is much evidence of increased engagement in social issues by the business sector in Latin America despite an historical absence of a culture of corporate community involvement. Recent studies in Brazil, Chile, and Ecuador demonstrate that the level of commitment of enterprises (both intellectual and in terms of resources) to community development is higher than official figures might suggest.[4]

---

[2] United Nations Development Program, *Human Development Report 1998* (New York: Oxford University Press, 1998), p. 206.

[3] Enrique V. Iglesias, *Reflexiones Sobre el Desarrollo Económico* (Washington, D.C.: Banco Inter-Americano de Desarrollo, 1992), p. 159. Translation by the authors.

[4] See, for instance, Luiza Monica Assis da Silva, *A Filantropía Empresarial: Um Estudo Exploratorio de Algumas Fundações Metropolitanas de São Paulo* (Brasília, Brazil: Universidade de Brasilia, 1996); Daniel Gertsacov, *Chilean Benchmarking Group* (Washington, D.C.: Points of Light Foundation, 1998); and Fundacion Esquel Ecuador (FEE), *Responsabilidad Social: Una Empresa de Todos* (Quito, Peru: 1998).

"Civil society has become an active player in the national development arena, particularly for its ability to deliver social services effectively to marginalized populations and incrementally for its contributions to the policy debate."

EFFORTS TO FORGE PARTNERSHIPS

There undoubtedly is growing awareness by the private sector of its new social role given this historical context so as to ensure, in partnership with the state and civil society, a healthy and stable society that is consistent with the achievement of the sector's long-term objectives. The establishment in recent years of such organizations as the Mexican Center on Philanthropy (CEMEFI—Centro Mexicano de Filantropia), Grupo de Institutos, Fundações e Empresas (GIFE) and EMPRESA in Brazil, Colombia's Center on Philanthropy, and Peru 2021 underscores the increased awareness and importance of social engagement as an area of attention for the business community. Similarly, conferences on corporate citizenship have been held in several countries, among them Chile, Ecuador, and, most recently, Brazil. These and other such efforts as well as an array of community development activities by businesses are successfully raising awareness of corporate citizenship in Latin America.[5]

Its increasing volume and changing nature notwithstanding, the "philanthropy" practiced by most businesses in Latin America has yet to become widespread or to be undertaken in a professional and strategic manner. Frequently, such efforts are not based on consideration of a strategy for community development and the enterprise's role in supporting it, but rather they tend to be based on traditional or patronizing patterns of giving. For instance, the vast majority of these efforts continue to be based on religious

[5] For an overview of many such initiatives in Latin America and the Caribbean, see the Inter-American Foundation (IAF)'s *Grassroots Development Journal*, vol. 21, no. 2 (1998), focusing on social investment; *Formacion de Alianzas para el Desarrollo Sostenible*, a joint publication of IAF, the Prince of Wales Business Leaders Forum and Kvaerner de Mexico (1998); and Ariel Fiszbein and Pamela Lowden, *Working Together for a Change—Government, Civic, and Business Partnerships for Poverty Reduction in Latin America and the Caribbean*, EDI Learning Resources Series (Washington, D.C.: The World Bank, 1999). For examples in Argentina, see I. Remeseria, "Capitalismo Social" in *Apertura* (1997), p.70.

convictions, with individuals and enterprises donating approximately 50 percent of their contributions to religious organizations.[6] Consequently, they are undertaken in the absence of clear goals and priorities determined in partnership with other societal actors, particularly the potential beneficiaries, and they fail to leverage other community resources.[7]

CRITICAL ISSUES FOR FORGING PARTNERSHIPS

Despite significant advancements, therefore, the effective development of a culture of social responsibility in Latin America faces serious challenges. The following issues have been repeatedly identified as critical for advancing corporate citizenship in the region:

1. Overcoming a history and culture of civic disengagement inherited from centralized and authoritarian colonial regimes, and preserved through traditional political practices such as "caudillismo" and "populismo".[8] Alfonso Esguerra notes that, "The mercantilist political scheme introduced by the Conquistadors [based on an autocratic central government and megabureaucracies] in conjunction with the influence of the Catholic Church characterized by a hierarchical structure and strict discipline have shaped the idiosyncrasy of the Latin American, leaving him [or her] more prone to vertical and dependent social relations."[9] The study undertaken by Fundación Esquel Ecuador in 1998 found that 77 percent of the interviewees believed the state has primary responsibility for solving social problems.[10]
2. Mistrust and lack of confidence across sectors in Latin America continue to be very high, partially as a result of the region's relatively recent period of authoritarian rule. The Ecuador study

---

[6] Gertsacov, *Chilean Benchmarking Group.*

[7] See Gertsacov, *Chilean Benchmarking Group*, as well as Adrian Hodges and Nelson Stratta, "Building Competitiveness and Communities—the Strategy of the Prince of Wales Business Leaders Forum to Promote Responsible Business in Latin America" (work in progress).

[8] "Caudillismo" is a Latin American term for the "strong-man" style of leadership. "Populismo" tends to refer to vertical governing styles along the lines of corporativism.

[9] Alfonso Esguerra, "La Filantropia del Desarrollo," (speech) p. 8. Translation by authors.

[10] For an overview of the challenges presented by a culture of citizen disengagement, in addition to Esguerra, "La Filantropia del Desarrollo,", see Inter-American Democracy Network, *En el Marco de la Responsabilidad Social* (Santiago, Chile: Corporacion Participa, 1998) and FEE, *Responsabilidad Social: Una Empresa de Todos.* Translations by authors.

"Its increasing volume and changing nature notwithstanding, the 'philanthropy' practiced by most businesses in Latin America has yet to become widespread or to be undertaken in a professional and strategic manner."

states it clearly: "Actors coincide in their objectives . . . but reveal a level of ignorance and prejudice regarding the other sector which makes the strengthening of civil society very difficult."[11]

3. Despite the advances noted above, corporate engagement continues to be identified with a few organizations, many of which are multinationals, and in most countries there is little indication of established capacity on which to base expansion. The Chilean Benchmarking Group (CBG) study notes that in Chile "many businesses lack the knowledge, experience, and developed networks to heighten the size and impact of their contributions."[12]
4. Similarly, there appears to be limited capacity within civil society to take a leading role in promoting and guiding the engagement of the private for-profit sector in the social arena. Despite increased awareness about the topic, in most of Latin America and the Caribbean traditional civil society organizations seem to be reacting slowly to this emerging trend. Preliminary results from a study on corporate giving in Brazil suggests that intermediary and grassroots nongovernmental organizations, for the most part, do not feel they are capable of engaging corporations in their action or fundraising strategies in a significant manner.[13] More important, in few countries have civil society organizations come together to analyze the sector's role in collaboration with the state and private sector and to design strategies for effectively assuming it.[14]

[11] FEE, *Responsabilidad Social: Una Empresa de Todos*, p. 22.

[12] Gertasov, *Chilean Benchmarking Group*, p. 41.

[13] Fundacao Grupo Esquel Brazil, "Philanthropy in Ceara" (unpublished).

[14] There are notable exceptions, such as the *Foro del Sector Social* in Argentina, whose objectives include, "foster efficient and transparent information systems as well as mechanisms for cooperation amongst public purpose organizations and the governmental and private sectors for social purposes". (*Tercer Sector* website, <http://www.tercersector.org.ar/foro/foro.htm>, as accessed on June 29, 1999).

5. Outdated and bureaucratic legal and regulatory frameworks, along with corruption, limit corporate engagement substantially. In Ecuador, 60 percent of business representatives think that the current legal framework is irrelevant to the promotion of philanthropy, while 16 percent think it actually undermines it.[15] The 1997 study entitled Marco Regulador para las Organizaciones de la Sociedad Civil concludes that, "The revision of laws and rules is urgently needed to achieve an adequate and consistent regulatory framework [for the strengthening of civil society]."[16]

OPPORTUNITIES FOR INTERVENTION

These issues highlight potential opportunities for critical intervention in the promotion of corporate citizenship in Latin America. One country is attempting to address these challenges through an innovative mechanism of collaboration between the private sector, the state, and civil society. The main purpose of the Instituto para la Promocion de la Empresa Social—IPES (Institute for the Promotion of Social Enterprise) being proposed in Uruguay is to promote organized participation by both citizens and enterprises, and to facilitate their relationship with each other and the state in addressing social problems.[17] The institute was envisioned by a multisectoral task force constituted by a group of Uruguayan leaders and the president of Uruguay in the context of the Reform and Modernization of the State Project, which was supported by the Inter-American Development Bank (IDB). The project, which sought to strengthen the relationship between the state and the citizen, has redefined the distribution of responsibilities among the three sectors. The IPES will provide the opportunity for civil society and the private sector to accompany the process of modernization of the state by building their own capacity to work together in addressing social issues. By doing so, it will enable constructive dialogue between the sectors and has the potential of signifi-

[15] FEE, *Responsabilidad Social: Una Empresa de Todos*, p. 26.

[16] Esquel Group Foundation, Inter-American Development Bank, International Center for Not-for-profit Law, *Marco Regulador para las Organizaciones de la Sociedad Civil* (Washington, D.C.: Inter-American Development Bank, 1998), p. 34.

[17] The Institute has received the support of the Inter-American Development Bank, the United Nations Development Program and the World Bank. For a detailed review see Nelson Stratta, "Instituto de Promocion de la Sociedad Civil," submitted to the Kellogg Foundation's Leaders in Philanthropy program.

"The IPES will provide the opportunity for civil society and the private sector to accompany the process of modernization of the state by building their own capacity to work together in addressing social issues."

cantly increasing the impact and efficiency of public social investment. The institute has defined the following as its potential areas of action:

- Promote an enabling legal framework and the appropriate mechanisms to facilitate interaction among the state, civil society, and the market in social projects.
- Act as a liaison between the state and civil society to facilitate the sector's development and to advance citizen participation in the design and implementation of public policy.
- Build the capacity of civil society organizations (CSOs), promoting their increased professionalism so as to enhance their effectiveness in tackling social issues in partnership with other sectors.
- Foster a national culture of citizen participation and a commitment to social responsibility.
- Support the private for-profit sector in efforts to engage in social activities.
- Promote knowledge management and creation so as to enhance the ability of all sectors to work together in achieving these common goals.
- Disseminate relevant information across sectors.

CONCLUSIONS

It remains to be seen whether the IPES will become viable in practice. Even in a small and relatively homogeneous country like Uruguay, the complex nature of this effort makes IPES and the partnerships it envisions vulnerable to political, economic, financial, and human factors, leading to delays in its implementation. Thus far, however, its existence as a collaborative project demonstrates both the ability of the private sector in Uruguay to grasp its new role and its determination to seek the necessary tools and mechanisms to assume it in collaboration with the state and civil society.

The Uruguay case illustrates the potential for innovative and collaborative responses to the serious challenges posed by the current economic, political, and social circumstances in Latin America. It also highlights the difficulties and limitations that might characterize collaboration among the state, civil society, and business sectors. While there seems to be a clear appreciation on the part of the Latin American corporate world of the need to have a stronger commitment to social well-being and to be part of sincere efforts to put that into practice, the region still faces important obstacles to fostering an effective culture of social responsibility. A traditionally disengaged civic culture, historical tensions across sectors, limited capacity, and unfavorable regulatory environments limit the likelihood of Latin American countries becoming "healthy societies," defined by Laurie Regelbrugge in this book as requiring "that corporate, civil society and government actors find appropriate ways to interact, collaborate, and exercise their respective independent roles."

In conclusion, Latin America is at a critical juncture when the need and potential for corporate engagement in social issues, in association with organizations of civil society, are very high and would constitute key aspects of a broader sense of responsible citizenship in the region. May the "continent of hope" thrive in opportunity by seriously addressing its current shortcomings.

Nelson Stratta is president of Grupo Esquel Uruguay and an associate consultant to the Prince of Wales Business Leaders Forum. An industrial engineer, he acts as an international consultant to both private firms and multilateral organizations, including the United Nations Development Program, the Inter-American Development Bank, the World Bank, the government of Uruguay, the government of Argentina, the government of Bolivia, the government of Colombia, the South-North Development Initiative, the African Development Bank, the Malaysian Ministry for Tourism, and Booz Allen and Hamilton. Mr. Stratta has worked in Argentina, Brazil, Bolivia, Chile, Colombia, Malaysia, the European Union, and the United States. He received an M.Sc. in management from the Imperial College of Science and Technology in London and a Ph.D. from Fraunhofer Institute for Innovation Research in Karlsruhe, Germany.

Marisol Pagés is executive director of the Esquel Group Foundation (EGF), where she is responsible for the technical assistance, design, and development of projects for Grupo Esquel; financial and institutional management of EGF; and the coordination of U.S. and international conferences and meetings. Ms. Pagés has a strong background in private sector management in both the United States and the Dominican Republic. She was U.S. director for syndication for Jenevis Marketing Limited. After returning to the Dominican Republic, she became chief financial officer and vice president for New Business for Pagés/BBDO, one of the top advertising agencies in the country. As research analyst for the American Chamber of Commerce of the Dominican Republic, she prepared the report "Analysis of the Enterprise for the Americas Initiative (EAI): Implications for the Dominican Republic," which was used by the Dominican delegation at the U.S. congressional hearings on EAI. Ms. Pagés has a B.A., cum laude, in economics and international political economy from the University of Wisconsin. She currently is pursuing an M.A. in international development at American University.

An Initiative to Promote Corporate Engagement in North America

8

Peter Shiras and Roberto Senderowitsch

BACKGROUND

CIVICUS North America includes Canada, Mexico, and the United States. While developing the regional action plan, many of the organization's advisory committee members noted that corporate citizenship is an issue that CIVICUS North America (CNA) is well suited to explore. The rationale for addressing corporate citizenship is threefold. First, attention is merited because of the preponderance of global corporations based in the region. Second, each of the three countries has several programs focused on corporate citizenship, so there is a growing body of relevant knowledge and experience. Finally, the specific dynamics of corporate engagement in the three countries themselves—their similarities, differences, and broader implications—merit attention. The region represents an opportunity to explore the question of what roles the nonprofit, business, and government sectors can play in building an effective regional framework for promoting effective corporate citizenship practices.

While some corporations show an extraordinarily high social commitment to their country of origin, they do not automatically replicate this behavior in other countries where they operate. This is particularly true in developing countries, where a company's standard of behavior is often far below practice in its home country. Therefore, a paradox is created in which one company can be an example for corporate citizenship in one country and a model to avoid in another.

In October 1998 approximately fifty-five CNA members defined a regional action plan. The development of a regional project to increase the level of corporate engagement in social affairs was assigned a high priority. CNA identified several reasons for and factors to consider in undertaking a regional strategy on corporate citizenship in North America.

- Companies working internationally cannot be partially responsible socially. They should implement their programs consistently in all the countries where they conduct their operations.
- Corporations and nonprofit organizations can learn from partnerships conducted in other countries of the region.
- Regulations and administrative barriers may prevent companies from engaging in corporate philanthropy activities internationally. Likewise, tax or other incentives may create a strong enabling environment for corporate social engagement in certain countries.
- The role of pressure groups and consumer attitudes should also be examined as a factor influencing corporate social engagement and potentially leading to differential corporate behavior in a national, as opposed to transnational, context.
- In the context of increasing regional cooperation in which the North American Free Trade Agreement was created, the development of a regional framework to link corporations to social causes is needed.

By developing a regional framework in corporate citizenship, CNA seeks to contribute to the global CIVICUS Corporate Engagement Initiative and also to achieve goals that relate to CIVICUS's three priorities: convening, collecting and disseminating knowledge and information, and advocacy.

CIVICUS North America is organizing forums in which corporate, government, and nonprofit actors from the three countries can meet to create and pursue opportunities for three-party partnerships. Because members have access to hundreds of organizations in the region, CIVICUS North America constitutes an effective channel of communication among its members, other NGOs, the government, the corporate sector, and the general public. Successful practices, research reports, and common concerns can easily be disseminated through the network.

The broad network of members and their constituents also represents the opportunity for CNA members to become a powerful voice of the third sector regionally. In a context of increasing integration, in which national economies tend to be globalized, national policies might have a significant impact on neighboring countries. Therefore, by constituting a "regional front" the third sector might be able to influence governments to ease the barriers for cross-national corporate citizenship initiatives.

CNA'S CORPORATE CITIZENSHIP GOALS

CIVICUS North America has several specific goals for its corporate citizenship initiatives.

- ***To identify barriers to increased corporate engagement in the three countries***—Barriers might be legal and regulatory issues, they might relate to the demand for corporate social responsibility in each country, or they might be influenced by the business operating climate in each country or by other factors.
- ***To promote the creation of incentives for corporations***—Corporations might receive financial incentives such as tax exemptions when contributing to social causes in neighboring countries. This policy approach might increase the level of corporate giving.
- ***To erase barriers that prevent companies from acting regionally***—Companies restricted by national laws might be willing to conduct philanthropic actions regionally. Eliminating barriers might increase the level of corporate involvement in social issues.
- ***To assess the desirability of developing a set of regional standards***—A set of standards might be developed to orient the philanthropic and community-oriented action of corporations that operate in the region. These standards might include issues of accountability and ethics.

ACTIVITIES

CNA is conducting research to identify barriers to enhanced corporate engagement and to identify incentives that would be effective on a regional level. Much of this research will draw on existing information. The International Center for Not-for-Profit Law will be one resource contributing to the effort as will be the Imagine program of the Canadian Centre for Philanthropy and the Corporate Engagement program of the Mexican Center for Philanthropy. In addition, the effort will draw on numerous initiatives taking place in the United States, including a new effort by Independent Sector on corporate-nonprofit partnerships.

CNA is planning to organize a conference—possibly in conjunction with a major meeting held by Business for Social Responsibility, the Independent Sector, the Canadian Centre for Philanthropy, or the Mexican Center for Philanthropy—to increase the level of exchange of information and to share successful practices of cross-border corporate citizenship and partnerships.

CNA members understand their potential role and opportunities for being effective vehicles for informing government officials about the needs of the third sector. The softening of regulatory barriers and the creation of financial incentives may be key elements in increasing the level of corporate citizenship in the region.

> *"The region represents an opportunity to explore the question of what roles the nonprofit, business, and government sectors can play in building an effective regional framework for promoting effective corporate citizenship practices."*

Corporate philanthropy is a relatively new field. Corporations use various mechanisms to promote their social agenda, such as cause-related marketing, gifts in kind, and grants. However, this field requires and offers a great amount of creativity and ingenuity. Success stories and best practices of initiatives operating in the North American region will contribute to the achievement of project goals and to the advancement of corporate citizenship in, and possibly beyond, the region.

To disseminate useful information about corporate initiatives, research, results, and policy issues, CNA will rely on the existing publications and networks of members.

CONCLUSION

CIVICUS North America is well positioned to contribute positively to corporate citizenship practice through its investigation of how corporate citizenship is implemented within and across the three countries in North America. The initiative will explore the activities of large, medium, and small companies. It will also review the legal and regulatory frameworks that influence corporate citizenship in each of the three countries. Finally, this effort will gather information from nonprofit organizations about their partnerships with the business sector within a given country and across borders and about their cross-border partnerships with other nonprofits.

The initiative will yield valuable information about how the third sector can be strengthened through its involvement with counterparts in other countries and through its attention to corporate citizenship and the regulatory framework in which companies and nonprofits operate.

Peter Shiras is senior vice president for programs at Independent Section (IS), a nonprofit coalition of over seven hundred corporate, foundation, and voluntary organization members. He oversees the programs for research, government relations, leadership, and communications. Before join-

ing IS, Mr. Shiras was vice president and director of government relations and public outreach of InterAction, an association of international relief and development organizations. Additionally, he spent thirteen years at Catholic Relief Services (CRS), working in several senior positions in Central America and East Africa, directing programs in Latin America and the Caribbean, and in Africa; and directing public policy and relations with the U.S. Congress, the United Nations, and the World Bank. Mr. Shiras also worked for the Inter-American Development Bank, the Institute for Science and Appropriate Technology of the Guatemalan Ministry of Agriculture, and as a consultant to Oxfam-U.K. in Guatemala. He is fluent in Spanish and has published numerous articles and several chapters in books. His op-ed articles have appeared in the "New York Times," the "Washington Post," the "Christian Science Monitor," and the "Baltimore Sun." He received both B.S. and M.S. degrees in agricultural economics from Cornell University.

Roberto Senderowitsch is assisting CIVICUS North America to develop its corporate citizenship initiative. He is pursuing a Master's degree in policy studies at the Johns Hopkins University where he is also an International Philanthropy Fellow with the Center of Civil Society Studies. He has worked at the Multilateral Investment Fund of the Inter-American Development Bank, planning job training courses and policies for Latin American and Caribbean countries. He spent two years in Cuba as the field representative for the American Jewish Joint Distribution Committee, and has worked for almost ten years in nonprofit organizations running educational and cultural programs. Mr. Senderowitsch has also served as a human resources consultant for several multinational companies including Telecom (telecommunications), Siderar (metallurgy), and Tecpetrol (oil). He was born in Buenos Aires, Argentina, and has his B.A. from the Universidad of Buenos Aires.

Business and Civil Society Organizations: Toward a New Partnership

9

Christopher Pinney

For most of the past fifty years, there has been relatively little relationship between civil society organizations (CSOs) and business. In most countries, the dominant role of the state in shaping economic and social development meant that there was little need for a direct connection between the voluntary and private sectors. Any existing positive relationship between these two sectors has focused primarily on the philanthropic activities of a relatively small group of companies. More frequently, however, CSO-business relations have tended to focus on the negative effects of business on society, and they often have been highly adversarial in nature. There has been little shared experience working on common goals that would lead to higher levels of understanding and trust between CSOs and business.

Today, both CSOs and business are being challenged to define a common agenda and to develop a much more constructive framework for engagement with each other. Global economic and social restructuring in the last decade has created a new landscape in which the "old" social contract between the public, private, and voluntary sectors—the traditional and existing division of labor among sectors—no longer meets society's needs. Locally, nationally, and globally we see the search for a new social contract in which responsibility for a society's well-being and development is more equally shared between business, CSOs, and governments. The forces driving these changes include the diminished legitimacy and capacity of the nation state, the dominance of global economic forces, and increased expectations for both business and CSOs to take greater responsibility for society's well-being.

For business, growing expectations for "social responsibility" are rapidly becoming a key strategic issue, particularly for large multinationals. In the new global society, simply operating within the law is no longer sufficient to manage public expectations for corporate social performance. To start with, there are few credible global laws or standards; and, more important, thanks to the power of new information technologies, CSOs as public interest advocates now have the power to call business to public account on social responsibility issues at a global level.

Some of the world's most successful companies, including Shell, Nike, Union Carbide, Monsanto, and Exxon, operating entirely within the law, have in the last decade experienced devastating public relations disasters as a result of negative public perceptions of their handling of social responsibility. These incidents have seriously hurt the reputation and credibility of these companies and, correspondingly, have hurt shareholder value. At the same time, many leadership companies are beginning to understand that being a good corporate citizen has direct and tangible benefits. A reputation as a good citizen can be a key asset in attracting and keeping customers, opening new markets, and attracting and retaining a loyal and productive work force.

In response to the challenges of this new environment, leadership companies are now moving to adopt a new management model. This "stakeholder" model moves away from an exclusive focus on shareholders and customers toward a more active strategy to understand, manage, and measure the impact of a company's operations on a variety of key stakeholders, including workers, communities, suppliers, and others. It is this kind of stakeholder management thinking that is driving business involvement in a wide variety of initiatives seeking to build relationships between business and society. The initiatives include groups working at the international level, such as the Prince of Wales Business Leaders Forum, the Caux Round Table, and the World Bank Business Partners for Development program. A growing range of national-level initiatives have also been launched, such as Business in the Community (U.K.), Philippine Business for Social Progress, Business for Social Responsibility (USA), and Imagine's Caring Company program (Canada).

For CSOs, building a new relationship with business is also rapidly becoming a priority. There are two main reasons for this. The first and most pragmatic reason is that, faced with diminished resources from the state and increasing numbers of CSOs, the sector is increasingly looking to business as a source of financial resources to support its work. More important, forward-thinking CSOs now realize that many of the crucial issues they seek to address in building stronger communities and societies simply cannot be addressed without the active cooperation and participation of the private sector. Even in the world's most prosperous countries, CSOs and governments alone no longer have the legitimacy or capacity to be the sole determiners or supporters of social development. In Canada, for example, the federal government has cut 25 percent of transfers for human services to individuals in a five-year period. China has said that it will not establish old-age pensions and that people will have to fend for themselves.

> *"In the new global society, simply operating within the law is no longer sufficient to manage public expectations for corporate social performance. To start with, there are few credible global laws or standards; and, more important, thanks to the power of new information technologies, CSOs as public interest advocates now have the power to call business to public account on social responsibility issues at a global level."*

We are at a moment in history then when there is both the potential and the necessity to build a new "social contract" among business, governments, and CSOs. There is the possibility to create a much more synergistic and collaborative relationship between the three sectors. Whether this potential will be realized is far from certain. Decades of distrust and misunderstanding will need to be overcome. Fundamental changes in organizational culture and management practices of all three sectors will need to occur. Leadership and risk taking on new forms of partnership and social entrepreneurship need to be explored.

There are positive signs that we may be on the right road. At both the national and international levels there is rapid growth in the number of "intermediary" organizations working to build new relationships between business and the community. In the survey Imagine recently completed for CIVICUS on the global landscape for corporate citizenship, which is discussed in chapter 3 of this book, we identified more than one hundred significant initiatives working to build new partnerships between business, CSOs, and government for community and social development.

In Canada we have spent a decade encouraging corporate giving and volunteering through the Canadian Centre for Philanthropy's Imagine Caring Company Program. More than four hundred and fifty Canadian businesses, including many of the country's largest firms, are now committed to giving a minimum of 1 percent of their pretax profit to charity and to encouraging employee volunteering and giving. During the period Imagine has operated, we have seen corporate giving in Canada increase by over one billion dollars (Canadian), in constant dollars. Despite this achievement, we know that corporate giving alone is not the solution. We need a much more active engagement of business as a partner with CSOs in finding new solutions to the problems we face. We need businesses as actively engaged participants not simply as passive supporters. To this end, Imagine has just completed a year-long review with its members and has developed a new vision for corporate citizenship in Canada. This vision is outlined in *More Than Charity: A New Agenda for Canadian Corporate Citizenship*, which sets out an aggressive program to increase significantly business participation in social development in Canada.

We know from our research with CIVICUS that our experience in Canada is far from unique. Many other corporate philanthropy initiatives are evolving in similar ways. The challenge and the opportunity now are to link the many initiatives going on globally so that we can more effectively learn from each other, reinforce and strengthen our programs, and catalyze new initiatives in countries where this process is not yet under way. Working with the UN, World Bank, and other multilateral agencies we need to make sure corporate engagement is a central issue on both national and global development agendas.

Through the CIVICUS Corporate Engagement Project and participation in the World Bank's Business Partners for Development Program, CIVICUS is exploring how it can be a catalyst and a leader in this regard. The challenge now is to engage the broader CIVICUS membership in this discussion. Over the next year, starting with the World Assembly in Manila, CIVICUS members will have an opportunity to participate in developing a series of initiatives under consideration for CIVICUS's corporate engagement work. Several options for the next phase of CIVICUS action exist.

- Initiatives designed to explore the creation of leadership standards for corporate citizenship globally;
- Forums and roundtables to address both the potential and issues to be addressed in business-CSO partnerships; and
- Capacity-building activities to assist CIVICUS's CSO members to increase their skills and abilities to engage business at the local, national, and regional levels.

In making decisions about which are the most appropriate activities to undertake, CIVICUS will continue to draw on the experience of its members in pursuing opportunities to strengthen civil society. Engaging corporations is as strategic for CSOs as it is for businesses and governments.

Christopher Pinney is director of Imagine and vice president for corporate citizenship at the Canadian Centre for Philanthropy in Toronto. He serves as coordinator for the CIVICUS Corporate Engagement Project. More biographical information appears at the end of chapter 3.

Aspirations for Advancing Corporate Citizenship in the Next Millennium

10

Rajesh Tandon

As we approach the new millennium, there has been a greater acknowledgment of the role of business institutions in promoting economic development and growth in society. The place of the modern corporation as an integral part of society, the diversification of its roles, the spread of corporations into a variety of economic activities, and the expansion in their legitimacy are only going to increase in the next millennium. It is in this context that we need to explore the meaning of corporate citizenship.

Historically, numerous businesses and corporate leaders have supported societal causes over the last hundred years through charitable contributions and direct involvement. In India, for example, notable support came during the freedom struggle under the leadership of Mahatma Gandhi. After independence, Indian private corporate enterprise remained a second fiddle to the public sector, at least in policy pronouncements and with respect to legitimacy in public eyes.

In today's context, we acknowledge and accept that modern business institutions must be efficient and profitable. We see them as engines of economic development and generators of wealth for the society. In light of the expansion in their roles and legitimacy in global society, businesses need to pay attention to the concept of corporate citizenship. The whole notion of citizenship implies that they are accorded certain rights and are at the same time responsible for meeting certain obligations to the society at large.

Businesses need "a license to operate" and they need public acceptance. To secure and maintain these they must abide by laws and regulations governing their operations, and they must conduct their work in a manner that fosters public trust. When this public trust is violated, whether deliberately through negligence or unintentionally, companies often lose their capacity to thrive or even survive.

Five broad themes of corporate citizenship appear to be relevant to our aspirations for corporate citizenship in the new millennium. These themes relate to the variety of stakeholders that modern corporations interact with in the course of conducting their normal, daily business.

THE BUSINESS ENTERPRISE AS AN INSTITUTION OF SOCIETY

First, corporate citizenship implies the development of business enterprises as modern institutions of society. In this institutional context, they must demonstrate societally relevant values in labor relations and human resource development. They must have a high standard of workplace safety and health. They must practice and promote transparent, accountable governance mechanisms in their own decisionmaking, and they must be law-abiding citizens within the single or many countries in which they do business. With democratic governance on the rise throughout the world, we would expect corporations increasingly to evolve norms and practices, cultures, and systems that reflect and express democratic values in model corporate institutions.

HOW BUSINESS RELATES TO CUSTOMERS

A second aspect of corporate citizenship is the relationship with consumers. Serving customers demands attention to and ever-improving quality, pricing, and delivery of products and services. Consumers also expect businesses to use innovative technology in their production of goods. Because society is also a consumer of corporate products and services, standards of excellence in quality, competitive pricing, and appropriate, new applications of relevant technology have to be established as guidelines and benchmarks for assessing corporate citizenship. Increasingly, consumers are demanding that the production processes adopted by companies meet high quality standards, or minimize adverse effects, with respect to their impact on workers, communities, and the natural environment.

BUSINESS AS A MEMBER OF THE COMMUNITY

A third and increasingly important area of consideration in corporate citizenship relates to the communities—the physical locations—where the economic activities are undertaken. This aspect of corporate citizenship is often the most contentious, providing a setting for conflict and difference of opinion on issues of ownership, rights, responsibilities, and decisionmaking authority. When and where factories are constructed, mines opened, and hotels built,

> *"This prospect demands that corporate citizenship take on the most critical challenges in development. It calls for a contribution from corporate citizens to insert themselves in the processes and institutions trying to address the profound problems of poverty, hunger, illiteracy, and ill health, all of which are evident in society today."*

there are always issues of acquiring land and other resources (water, forests, and minerals, for example) on which some communities and families depend for their subsistence and survival.

To use again the example of India, a large, thickly populated country, creating space for and directing resources to a business necessarily means taking them away from or substantially reducing their use by some community groups or others. In such circumstances, many social activists and nongovernmental voluntary organizations have come forward to help articulate the demands and concerns of displaced communities. Corporate responses in recent years, as seen from incidents in southern Orissa and western Maharashtra, have shown a high-handedness and blind pursuit of narrow economic interest, without any consideration for the impact on or survival of those who have been displaced.

These issues need to be addressed within a larger national and global perspective, keeping the cost and benefit of development over displacement of people in a proper balance and in full view. Assuring a sustainable livelihood and a life of dignity for those who are displaced from resources hitherto accessible to them has to be integral to enlightened corporate citizenship today and in the future.

By the same token, we must acknowledge and encourage companies that pursue promising practices in their community efforts—those whose actions contribute substantially to improving the health and well-being of community residents. Companies that participate with public sector and community actors to provide clean water, health care services, high quality education, housing, safe employment, and transitional support when they shift operations out of communities are contributing to economic development and community infrastructure that residents need.

SUSTAINING THE ENVIRONMENT

A fourth theme is that enlightened corporate citizenship requires paying attention to the life sustaining, regenerative capacity of our ecology. We as citizens and companies as corporate citizens must make use of forest, land, mineral, air, and water resources in ways that ensure they are regenerated, revitalized, and available for successive future generations. That is the meaning of sustainability. A fundamental concern for environmental sustainability must enter into long-term, strategic corporate planning and it must also be tangible in short-term operations, business decisions, and accounting.

This is not merely a question of meeting the minimum requirements of laws. It is essentially a question of perspective and commitment to future generations. The manner in which effluents are left in the environment and the manner in which natural resources are exploited in extreme ways for short-term gain leave much to be desired. Enlightened corporate citizenship would expect high standards of ecological sensitivity and deliberate inclusion in all forms of corporate decisionmaking: for example, in sourcing raw materials; in selecting technologies in production; and in choosing methods of storing, transporting, and marketing products and services.

EXCLUDED POPULATIONS

Finally, our global society and many individual countries today face the serious problem of the societal exclusion of large portions of the population. These people are outside the framework of the global economy. They lack basic education and the skills needed to participate effectively as producers or citizens in the economy and society, and they lack purchasing power and economic capacity to be influential consumers. This large-scale exclusion of large numbers of citizens from the modern economy, which in some countries applies to more than half the population, is not sustainable in the long run. If large segments of the population remain excluded, the mainstream itself will become marginalized or redundant.

This prospect demands that corporate citizenship take on the most critical challenges in development. It calls for a contribution from corporate citizens to insert themselves in the processes and institutions trying to address the profound problems of poverty, hunger, illiteracy, and ill health, all of which are evident in society today. It is not merely the financial or monetary contributions of companies that can bring about desired positive change; modern corporate institutions have enormous intellectual, human, and creative capacities. Their managerial talent and professional expertise are so vast that the application and dedication of these to the processes and institutions addressing the most pressing problems of our society would make a dramatic and significant contribution to solutions in the future.

"We as citizens and companies as corporate citizens must make use of forest, land, mineral, air, and water resources in ways that ensure they are regenerated, revitalized, and available for successive future generations. That is the meaning of sustainability."

A MANDATE FOR ENGAGEMENT

Our aspirations for the corporate citizenship described above cannot be delivered by corporations alone. These achievements require the direct involvement of citizens, civil society, and governments. For companies to advance their labor relations and workforce practices, they need dedicated employees and outside scrutiny to accompany and complement managerial talent in highlighting areas for improvement. Effective customer service requires that we listen to customers and potential customers about their needs and aspirations and that we learn their concerns and misgivings. Being a good corporate citizen in the communities where a business operates means establishing relationships with the full range of people and institutions affected by business operations. Positive relations within communities yield the license to operate that is essential for business success. Preserving our natural environment and the diverse ecosystems on the planet requires a commitment to sustainable practices. This applies to companies, to all other institutions, and to private citizens. Finally, addressing those who are excluded from the development process and seeking any corresponding benefits requires that we move outside our normal, comfortable networks, and that we dare to take risks.

All of these advancements in corporate citizenship require the involvement of all three sectors, sometimes working jointly and sometimes separately, sometimes through cooperation and other times through opposition. Likewise, all of these advancements and aspirations depend on the people involved and on their ability and commitment as they pursue their roles as citizens, workers, parents, and members of the general public. Corporate citizenship has been and always will be a function of the people involved who are making and implementing decisions. The same is true of the citizenship of all of our other public and private institutions.

As one who has been active with voluntary development organizations for twenty years, whose own professional background in engineering and management was applied to address the problems of the local communities, I have found this a worthwhile and challenging career. I am confident that many corporate leaders and managers understand the problems facing our society today and are committed to contribute their part in achieving positive change for our children. We want effectively performing and enlightened corporate citizens, institutions that, while making profit and generating wealth, are also aspiring to contribute substantially to improving the quality of life for one and all and preserving the health and vitality of our natural environment.

Rajesh Tandon is the founder and executive director of the Society for Participatory Research in Asia (PRIA), a nongovernmental organization based in New Delhi, India. He serves as chairperson of the CIVICUS Board of Directors (1997–99); as president of the Asia-South Pacific Bureau of Adult Education, an Asia Pacific regional NGO; and as an Asian vice president of the International Council for Adult Education. Dr. Tandon holds a Ph.D. in Organizational Behavior from Case Western Reserve University in Cleveland, Ohio. He has written extensively on participatory research and development strategies in the third world.

Resources on Business and Civil Society Engagement

This resource section is presented to assist those working on these subjects. It is not a comprehensive list, but we have sought to include contact information for the authors' organizations and provide information for other organizations working on these subjects. The authors' organizations are not repeated in the Organizational Resources Section.

AUTHORS' ORGANIZATIONS

Christopher Pinney and Maxwell Brem
Canadian Centre for Philanthropy
IMAGINE Program/Corporate Citizenship
425 University Avenue Suite 700
Toronto, Ontario
Canada M5G 1T6
Tel: (416) 597-2293
Fax: (416) 597-2294
www.ccp.ca/imagine

Kumi Naidoo, Laurie Regelbrugge, and Alina Zyszkowski
CIVICUS
World Alliance for Citizen Participation
919 18th Street NW, Third Floor
Washington, DC 20006
U.S.A.
Tel: (202) 331-8518
Fax: (202) 331-8774
www.civicus.org

Peter Shiras and Roberto Senderowitsch
CIVICUS North America
Independent Sector
1200 18th Street NW
Washington, DC 20036
U.S.A.
Tel: (202) 467-6100
Fax: (202) 467-6101
www.indepsec.org

Manuel Arango
CONCORD, S.A. De C.V.
Campos Eliseos 400 - PH 1
Mexico City 11000
Mexico
Tel: (525) 281-1516
Fax: (525) 280-2851

Marisol Pagés and Nelson Stratta
Esquel Group Foundation
1003 K Street NW, Suite 800
Washington, DC 20001-4425
U.S.A.
Tel: (202) 347-1796
Fax: (202) 347-1797
www.esquel.org

Tadashi Yamamoto
Japan Center for International Exchange
4-9-17, Minami Azabu Minato-ku
Tokyo 106-0047
Japan
Tel: (81) (3) 3346-7781
Fax: (81) (3) 3443-7580
www.jcie.or.jp

Ros Tennyson
Prince of Wales Business Leaders Forum
15-16 Cornwall Terrace
Regent's Park, London NW1 4QP
United Kingdom
Tel: (44)(171) 467-3656
Fax: (44)(171) 467-3610
www.oneworld.org/pwblf

AUTHORS' ORGANIZATIONS (continued)

Rajesh Tandon
Society for Participatory Research in Asia
42, Tughlakabad Institutional Area
New Delhi 110 062
India
Tel: (91) (11) 698-1908
Fax: (91) (11) 698-0183

Nigel Twose and Amanda Blakeley
World Bank Group
1818 H Street NW
Washington, DC 20433
U.S.A.
Tel: (202) 477-1234
www.worldbank.org
Business Partners for Development
www.worldbank.org/bpd

ORGANIZATIONAL RESOURCES

AIESEC International (global student network)
Teilingerstraat 110-128
Rotterdam NL-3032 AW
The Netherlands
Tel: (31)(10) 243-0603
Fax: (31)(10) 265-1386
www.aiesec.org

Apparel Industry Partnership
Bureau of International Labor Affairs
Department of Labor
200 Constitution Avenue NW
Washington, DC 20210
U.S.A.
Tel: (202) 219-6666
www.dol.gov/dol/ilab
No Sweat Initiative:
www.dol.gov/dol/esa/public/nosweat/nosweat.html

Asia Pacific Philanthropy Consortium
Asia Foundation
465 California Street, 14th Floor
San Francisco, CA 94104
U.S.A.
Tel: (415) 982-4640
Fax: (415) 392-8863
www.asiafoundation.org

Aspen Institute
45 Rockefeller Plaza, 7th Floor
New York, NY 10111
U.S.A.
Tel: (212) 218-5010
Fax: (212) 218-5012
www.aspeninst.org

Boston College
Center for Corporate Community Relations
Wallace E. Carroll School of Management
Chestnut Hill, MA 02467-3835
U.S.A.
Tel: (617) 552-4545
Fax: (617) 552-8499
www.bc.edu/cccr

Business Council for Sustainable Energy
1200 18th Street NW, 9th Floor
Washington, DC 20036
U.S.A.
Tel: (202) 785-0507
Fax: (202) 785-0514
www.bcse.org

Business Enterprise Trust
204 Junipero Serra Boulevard
Stanford, CA 94305
U.S.A.
Tel: (415) 321-5100
Fax: (415) 321-5774
www.betrust.org

Business for Social Responsibility
609 Mission Street, 2nd Floor
San Francisco, CA 94105-3506
U.S.A.
Tel: (415) 537-0888
Fax: (415) 537-0889
www.bsr.org
Global Business Responsibility Resource Center
www.bsr.org/resourcecenter

Business in the Community
44 Baker Street
London W1M 1DH
United Kingdom
Tel: (44)(171) 224-1600
Fax: (44)(171) 486-1700
www.bitc.org.uk

Business Partnership Unit
Department for International Development
94 Victoria Street
London SW1E 5JL
United Kingdom
Tel: (44)(171) 917-0380
Fax: (44)(171) 917-0797
www.dfid.gov.uk

Business Roundtable
1615 L Street NW
Washington, DC 20036
U.S.A.
Tel: (202) 872-1260
Fax: (202) 466-3509
www.brtable.org

Caux Round Table Secretariat
Amaliastraat 10
2514 JC The Hague
The Netherlands
Tel: (31)(70) 360-5260
Fax: (31)(70) 361-7209
www.caux.ch

Center for the Study of Ethics in the Professions
Illinois Institute of Technology
102 Stuart Building
10 West 31st Street
Chicago, IL 60616-3793
U.S.A.
Tel: (312) 567-3017
Fax: (312) 567-3016
www.iit.edu/~csep
Codes of Ethics Online:
http://csep.iit.edu/codes

Centre for Innovation in Corporate Responsibility
342 MacLaren Street
Ottawa, ON K2P OM6
Canada
Tel: (613) 276-6080
Fax: (613) 238-5642
www.cicr.net

Committee for Economic Development
2000 L Street NW
Washington, DC 20036
U.S.A.
Tel: (202) 296-5860
Fax: (202) 223-0776
www.ced.org

Conference Board
845 3rd Avenue
New York, NY 10022-6679
U.S.A.
Tel: (212) 759-0900
Fax: (212) 980-7014
www.conference-board.org

Co-Op America
1612 K Street NW, Suite 600
Washington, DC 20006
U.S.A.
Tel: (202) 872-5307
Fax: (202) 331-8166
www.coopamerica.org

The Corporate Citizenship Company
14 Soho Square
London W1V 5FB
Tel: (44) (171) 287-6676
Fax: (44) (171) 287-8139

Council on Foundations
1828 L Street NW
Washington, DC 20036
U.S.A.
Tel: (202) 466-6512
Fax: (202) 785-3926
www.cof.org

Ethical Trading Initiative
16 Baldwin's Gardens/S. 204
London ECIN 7RJ
United Kingdom
Tel: (44)(171) 831-8677
Fax: (44)(171) 405-5943
www.ethicaltrade.org

European Foundation Centre
51, Rue de la Concorde
Brussels B-1050
Belgium
Tel: (32)(2) 512-8938
Fax: (32)(2) 512-3265
www.efc.be

European Foundation for Quality Management
Avenue des Pleiades 15
1200 Brussels
Belgium
Tel: (32)(2) 775-3511
Fax: (32)(2) 775-3535
www.efqm.org

ORGANIZATIONAL RESOURCES (continued)

European Partners for the Environment
Rue Mounier 83-Box 1
1200 Brussels-Woluwe
Belgium
Tel: (32)(3) 312-9383
www.epe.be

Institute for Development Research
44 Farnsworth Street
Boston, Massachusetts
02210-1211
U.S.A.
Tel: (617) 422-0422
Fax: (617) 482-0617
www.jsi.com/idr/

Institute of Business Ethics
12 Palace Street
London SW1E 5JA
United Kingdom
Tel: (44)(171) 931-0495
Fax: (44)(171) 821-5819
www.ibe.org.uk

Institute of Social and Ethical AccountAbility
Vine Court/First Floor
112-116 Whitechapel Road
London E1 1JE
United Kingdom
Tel: (44)(171) 377-5866
Fax: (44)(171) 377-5720
www.accountability.org.uk

Instituto Ethos
Rua Francisco Leitao, 469
Conj. 1407-CEP 05414-020
Sao Paulo/SP
Brazil
Tel/Fax: (55)(11)3068-8539

Interfaith Center on Corporate Responsibility
475 Riverside Drive
New York, NY 10115
U.S.A.
Tel: (212) 870-2293
Fax: (212) 870-2023

International Accounting Standards Committee
166 Fleet Street
London EC4A 2DY
United Kingdom
Tel: (44)(171) 353-0565
Fax: (44)(171) 353-0562
www.iasc.org.uk
Description: Accounting organization

International Business Ethics Institute
1000 Connecticut Avenue NW, Suite 503
Washington, DC 20036
U.S.A.
Tel: (202) 296-6938
Fax: (202) 296-5897
www.business-ethics.org

International Chamber of Commerce
38, Cours Albert 1er
75008 Paris
France
Tel: (33)(1) 4953-2828
Fax: (33)(1) 4953-2859
www.iccwbo.org

International Development Research Centre (IDRC)
Mailing Address (IDRC)
PO Box 8500
Ottawa, ON K1G 3H9
Canada
Head office location (IDRC)
250 Albert Street
Ottawa, ON K1P 6M1
Canada
Tel: (613) 236 6163
www.idrc.ca

International Institute for Sustainable Development
161 Portage Avenue East
Winnipeg, Manitoba
Canada R3B OY4
Tel: (204) 958-7700
Fax: (204) 958-7710
http://iisd1.iisd.ca

International Labor Organization
4, route des Morillons
CH-1211 Geneva 22
Switzerland
Tel: (41)(22) 799-7456
www.ilo.org
ILO Declaration on Fundamental Principles and Rights at Work:
www.ilo.org/public

International Organization for Standardization
Central Secretariat
1, rue de Varembe
Case postale 56
CH-1211 Geneva 20
Switzerland
Tel: (41)(22) 749-0111
Fax: (41)(22) 733-3430
www.iso.ch

Keidanren
Japan Federation of Economic Organizations
Keidanran Kaikan, 1-9-4 Otemachi
Chiyoda Tokyo
Japan
Tel: (81)(3) 3279-1411
Fax: (81)(3) 5255-6255
www.keidanren.or.jp

Minnesota Center for Corporate Responsibility
1000 LaSalle Avenue, Suite 153
Minneapolis, MN 55403
U.S.A.
Tel: (651) 962-4120
Fax: (651) 962-4125
www.stthomas.edu/mccr
Description: promotes the Caux Principles

National Association of Manufacturers
1331 Pennsylvania Avenue NW
Washington, DC 20004
U.S.A.
Tel: (202) 637-3000
Fax: (202) 637-3182
www.nam.org

National Round Table on the Environment and the Economy
Canada Building
344 Slater Street, Suite 200
Ottawa, Ontario
Canada K1R 7Y3
Tel: (613) 992-7189
Fax: (613) 992-7385
www.nrtee-trnee.ca

New Academy of Business
3-4 Albion Place
Galena Road
London W6 0LT
United Kingdom
Tel: (44)(181) 563-8780
Fax: (44)(181) 563-8618
www.new-academy.ac.uk

PACT
1901 Pennsylvania Avenue NW, Fifth Floor
Washington, DC 20006
U.S.A.
Fax: (202) 466-5669
www.pactworld.org

Partners In Change
E-270, Greater Kailash-II, Ground Floor
New Delhi-110 048
India
Tel/Fax: 011- 6233525, 64 18885, 6418887
E-mail: pic@actionaidindia.og
www.actionaidindia.org

Philanthropy Australia
111 Collins Street, Level 3
Melbourne, Victoria 3000
Australia
Tel: (61-3) 9650-9255
Fax: (61-3) 9654-8298

Philippine Business for Social Progress
3/F PSDC Building
Magallenes Corner Real Streets
Intramuros, Manila
Philippines
Tel: (632) 527-7751
Fax: (632) 527-3743
www.pbsp.org.ph

ORGANIZATIONAL RESOURCES (continued)

President's Council on Sustainable Development
730 Jackson Place NW
Washington, DC 20503
U.S.A.
Tel: (202) 408-5296
Fax: (202) 408-6839
www.whitehouse.gov/PCSD

Socially Responsible Business Unit
Department for International Development
94 Victoria Street
London SW1E 5JL
United Kingdom
Tel: (44)(171) 917-7000
Fax: (44)(171) 917-0019
www.dfid.gov.uk

Social Investment Forum
1612 K Street NW, Suite 600
Washington, DC 20006
U.S.A.
Tel: (202) 872-5319
Fax: (202) 331-8166
www.socialinvest.org

Social Venture Network Europe
4 Great James Street
London WC1N 3DA
United Kingdom
Tel: (44)(171) 242-4990
Fax: (44)(171) 242-5010
www.svneurope.com

Social Venture Network
The Presideo
P.O. Box 29221
Thoreau Center for Sustainability
San Francisco, CA 94129
U.S.A.
Tel: (415) 561-6501
Fax: (415) 561-6435
www.svn.org

Synergos Institute
100 East 85th Street
New York, NY 10028
U.S.A.
Tel: (212) 517-4900
Fax: (212) 517-4815
www.synergos.org

Transparency International
Otto-Suhr-Allee 97-99
D-10585 Berlin
Germany
Tel: (49)(30) 343-8200
Fax: (49)(30) 34-70-39-12
www.transparency.de

United Nations Commission on Sustainable Development
UN Plaza, Room DC2-2270
New York, NY 10017
U.S.A.
Tel: (212) 963-0902
Fax: (212) 963-4260
www.un.org/esa/sustdev

United Nations Development Programme
One UN Plaza
New York, NY 10017
U.S.A.
Tel: (212) 906-6634
www.undp.org

United Nations Environment Programme
Industry and Environment
Tour Mirabeau
39-43 quai Andre Citroen
75 739 Paris Cedex 15
France
Tel: (33)(1) 4437-1450
Fax: (33)(1) 4437-1474
www.unepie.org

United Nations Program for Accountability and Transparency
UN Plaza, Room DC2-2270
New York, NY 10017
U.S.A.
Tel: (212) 906-5349
Fax: (212) 906-5023

World Business Council for Sustainable Development
160 Route de Florissant
CH-1231 Conches
Switzerland
Tel: (41)(22) 839-3100
Fax: (41)(22) 839-3131
www.wbcsd.ch

World Economic Forum
53 chemin des Hauts-Crets
1223 Cologny
Geneva
Switzerland
Tel: (41)(22) 869-1212
Fax: (41)(22) 786-2744
www.weforum.org

World Federation of Sporting Goods Industry
BP 480
Le Hameau CH 1936 Verbier
Switzerland
Tel: (41)(27) 775-3570
Fax: (41)(27) 775-3579
www.wfsgi.org
Description: adopted model code of conduct

RELATED WEBSITE RESOURCES

Business in the Community
www.bitc.organisation.uk

Business Partners for Development
www.worldbank.org/bpd

Global Business Responsibility Resource Center
www.bsr.org/resourcecenter

ILO Declaration on Fundamental Principles and Rights at Work:
www.ilo.org/public

Prince of Wales Business Leaders Forum
www.oneworld.organisation/pwblf/

Promoting the Model Business Principles
United States Department of State
www.state.gov/www/global/human_rights/business_principles.html

Sustainability Challenge Foundation
www.mit.edu/scf/

United States Agency for International Development
New Partnerships Initiative (NPI)
www.info.usaid.government/pubs/npi

United States Department of Labor
Education and Training Administration
Corporate Citizenship Resource Center
www.ttrc.doleta.gov/citizen/corphome.htm

United States Department of Commerce
Global Business Practices Initiative and Model Business Principles
www.ita.doc.gov/bgp

United States Department of Labor
Employment Standards Administration
No Sweat Initiative
www.dol.gov/dol/esa/public/nosweat/nosweat.htm